HISTORIC BARS OF CHICAGO

A guide to the 100 most historic neighborhood taverns, blues bars, jazz clubs, cocktail lounges, sports bars, nightclubs, bierstubes, rock & punk clubs, and dives of Chicago

Sean Parnell

FIRST EDITION

CHICAGO

HISTORIC BARS OF CHICAGO

Sean Parnell

Published May 2010 by:

lcp@lakeclaremont.com
www.lakeclaremont.com

Copyright © 2010 by Sean Parnell

Publisher's Cataloging-In-Publication Data
(Prepared by The Donohue Group, Inc.)

Parnell, Sean, 1973-
    Historic bars of Chicago : a guide to the 100 most historic neighborhood taverns, blues bars, jazz clubs, cocktail lounges, sports bars, nightclubs, bierstubes, rock & punk clubs, and dives of Chicago / Sean Parnell.

    p. : ill., maps ; cm.

    Includes index.
    ISBN: 978-1-893121-82-9

1. Bars (Drinking establishments)—Illinois—Chicago—Guidebooks. 2. Taverns (Inns)—Illinois—Chicago—Guidebooks. 3. Nightclubs—Illinois—Chicago—Guidebooks. 4. Chicago (Ill.)—Guidebooks. I. Title.

TX950.57.I3 P37 2010
647/.95773/11   2009927757

    14 13 12 11 10   10 9 8 7 6 5 4 3 2 1

Printed in Canada.

This book is dedicated to my wife, my love and my inspiration, Lina.

I would also like to extend special thanks to my parents, Lyle & Dolores Parnell, who have demonstrated surprising resilience in accepting their son as an urban barfly.

Publisher's Credits

Cover design by Edward J. Campbell Inc.

Large and small cover photo of the
California Clipper by Elizabeth Sattelberger.
Other cover photos by Sean Parnell.

Interior design and layout by Mike Wykowski.

Photos by Sean Parnell.

Pub crawl maps by Sean Parnell,
using Google Map data, courtesy of Google.

Editing and proofreading by Sharon Woodhouse.

Indexing by Sean Parnell and Rachael Patrick.

Table of Contents

ACKNOWLEDGMENTS

This book draws inspiration from all of the following: Tina Chung and the original Thursday Night Club; the incredible but true drinking stories of Dave Welton, Bob Warda, Marc La Guardia, and the Brits Mike Betts and "Nigel" (real name withheld to protect the guilty); Jerry Kelly and Mike Kennedy for many a night at bw3 and "beyond"; the Australian boozing connection of Simon Spong and Matt Nichol who were always up for a "bevie" and who foolishly love the Cubs as much as I do; Tom Warda and Keith Wilkins for their thought-provoking pub crawls like Robefest; the Chicago History Museum for the opportunity to host their inaugural historic pub crawls; ProQuest and the *Chicago Tribune* for their archives; Sharon Woodhouse and Lake Claremont Press for the opportunity to write this book; Jimmy Sottosanto and Keith McGorisk for the encouragement to make more of the Chicago Bar Project; and finally, Bob McGann, one of my oldest friends, even though he's a White Sox fan—this book and this city would not be the same without him, his antics, and his encyclopedic knowledge of Chicago.

I would also like to thank all those Chicago barflies that came before, including: Jory Graham, Kay Loring, Rick Kogan & Dr. Nightlife, Dennis McCarthy, David Hoekstra, Ryan Ver Berkmoes, all the people at *Barfly*, John McGrath, Gertrude Heckens, Lynne Friedman, Jeff Ruby, Matt Richmond and the writers of *The Tap*, and Jonathan Stockton—all of whom deserve recognition for capturing a part of Chicago's continuously evolving tavern culture within their own writing.

PREFACE

I love Chicago bars–all of them. Even the lowliest dive contains something redeeming, if only for a cold beer and a bartender who at least pretends to care. The purpose of this book is to provide a living history of the 100 most historic bars in the city and the top five in the suburbs. Because change happens, this book also recounts the top five bars that I miss the most. Keep in mind that the bars profiled in this book may not be around forever (though their endurance through the decades may decrease the likelihood of their going out of business), so phone first before your visit and be sure to enjoy them while you still can.

Sadly, not all historic Chicago taverns could be included in this book. Many lesser-known pubs from Chicago's past (e.g., Chipp Inn, Wertellia's Tavern, Bob Inn), some of the best bars to arise within the last 20 years (e.g., Map Room, Hopleaf, Duke of Perth), and those whose historic legacy resides in the buildings housing them (e.g., Ole St. Andrew's Inn, Motel Bar, Skylark), will all have to be saved for another time. These other pubs, and hundreds of others that will interest Chicago bar enthusiasts, are covered on my website www.chibarproject.com. Visit for additional historical information, a "Gone but not Forgotten" memorial section, and stories (not to be confused with fact) on bars written about here that just couldn't fit into the pages of this book.

The good news: this is but the first edition of *Historic Bars of Chicago*. If you think a watering hole is worthy of coverage here, if you know a good story about a Chicago bar of historic value, or if you just have something to say, please email me at parnellsf@chibarproject.com. I hope you enjoy this book even more than I did "researching" it. Cheers!

—Sean Parnell

"Between the curved steel of the El and the nearest Clark Street hockshop, between the penny arcade and the shooting gallery, between the basement gin-mill and the biggest juke in Bronzeville, the prairie is caught for keeps at last. Yet on nights when the blood-red neon of the tavern legends tether the arc-lamps to all the puddles left from last night's rain, somewhere between the bright carnival of the boulevards and the dark girders of the El, ever so far and ever so faintly between the still grasses and the moving waters, clear as a cat's cry on a midnight wind, the Pottawatomies mourn in the river reeds once more."

—Nelson Algren, *Chicago: City on the Make* (1951)

THE HISTORIC 100

17 WEST AT THE BERGHOFF

17 W. Adams St. (200S, 0W)
Chicago, IL 60603
(312) 427-3170

Website	www.theberghoff.com
Neighborhood	Loop
Open 'til & Cover	10pm; never a cover
Drinks	Berghoff Beer, bourbon, wine
Food	"Bistro" American, best of German
Music	Mainly the lip-smacking of patrons
Bar Type	German Restaurant, Beer Hall

The Berghoff was founded in 1898, but its history dates back to the mid-1800s when Herman Joseph Berghoff came to America from Germany. He built the Berghoff Brewery in 1887 in Fort Wayne, Indiana, and later ran a saloon tent during the World's Columbian Exposition of 1892–3 that commemorated the 400th anniversary of the discovery of the New World. The fair also featured Captain Frederick Pabst, hand-tying blue silk ribbons around each bottle. Berghoff continued his success from the fair by opening three saloons in Chicago (primarily to sell his own beer), one of which was located on the southeast corner of State & Adams streets. When the lease expired in 1898, this location moved next door where 17 West at the Berghoff now stands. The current building was constructed in 1872, a year after the Great Chicago Fire. Contrary to what you might expect from a lifetime brewer, Berghoff took the high road during Prohibition by brewing "Bergo Soda Pop" and serving food, thus establishing a reputation for delectable German fare. When the Volstead Act was repealed in 1933, Berghoff himself went to City Hall and obtained Chicago liquor permit No. 1, still on display. After countless wienerschnitzels and corned beef sandwiches were served, Berghoff announced that it would close on February 28, 2006—on the heels of Marshall Field's re-branding as Macy's, adding to the angst of Chicagoans fearing an erosion of the city's cultural identity. Fortunately, Berghoff's doors quickly re-opened as "17 West at the Berghoff" by Carlyn Berghoff, great-granddaughter of HJB. Renovations were kept minor,

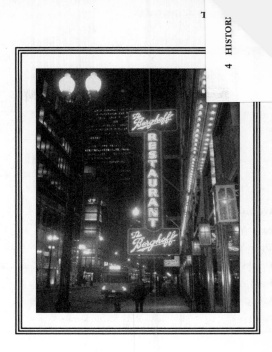

mainly an update of the menu and removal of the wall separating the bar from the dining room, making the room more spacious.

NEARBY	Miller's Pub – 134 S. Wabash Ave.
	Exchequer Pub – 226 S. Wabash Ave.
	The Gage – 24 S. Michigan Ave.
SIMILAR	**AUTHENTIC GERMAN TAVERNS**
	Chicago Brauhaus – 4732 N. Lincoln Ave.
	Resi's Bierstube – 2034 W. Irving Park Rd.
	Laschet's Inn – 2119 W. Irving Park Rd.
	OLD CHICAGO
	Schaller's Pump – 3714 S. Halsted St. (1881)
	Marge's Still – 1758 N. Sedgwick St. (1885)
	Green Mill – 4802 N. Broadway (1907)
TRIVIA	In what year did The Berghoff begin allowing female patrons?
NOTES	_____
	_____
	_____
	_____

ANSWER: 1969, following a stand-in organized by the National Organization for Women.

ABBEY PUB

3420 W. Grace St. (3800N, 3400W)
Chicago, IL 60618
(773) 478-4408

Website	www.abbeypub.com
Neighborhood	Irving Park
Open 'til & Cover	2am (3am Sat); $6–25 sports & music
Drinks	Jameson and a mean pint of Guinness
Food	A full traditional Irish menu
Music	Live folk & Sunday trad' sessions
Bar Type	Irish Pub, Music Venue

Since 1989, Abbey Pub has literally been run by Looneys… owners Tom and Bridget Looney that is, and they've done a fine job with the place. The crowds seem to grow bigger and more diverse each year, impressive considering that the Abbey Pub first opened its doors in 1973. Bridget once refused a pair of Irish lads from entering the bar to watch the football match between Dublin and Donegal without paying the cover charge. The pair just happened to be Bono and The Edge of U2, who wound up ponying up to get in. Step into the Abbey Pub and you're faced with a difficult choice. To your right is the 700-capacity party barn for live bands, mostly of the folk-rockabilly variety featured by the local label Bloodshot Records. Past performers include Neko Case, Waco Brothers, and Kris Kristofferson. Expect to pay a cover Thursday through Saturday. Otherwise, head to your left for a well-pulled pint of Guinness, and on weekends: Premier League Football (soccer), World Cup qualifying matches, 6-Nations Rugby, Gaelic football, and the bloody Irish sport of hurling. A lovely traditional Irish breakfast is served all day in the Lambay Island Dining Room on Sundays, complete with black and white pudding—if you don't know what's in them, don't ask. The Abbey Pub also hosts the longest running traditional Irish jam in the city, referred to as the "Irish Sessions," every Sunday at 8pm (no cover).

NEARBY   Independence Tap – 3932 W. Irving Park Rd.
Mirabell Restaurant & Lounge –
   3454 W. Addison St.
Chief O'Neill's Pub – 3471 N. Elston Ave.

SIMILAR   **THE BIG FOLKSY**
Schubas Tavern – 3159 N. Southport Ave.
Martyrs' – 3855 N. Lincoln Ave.
Hideout – 1354 W. Wabansia Ave.
A MEAN PINT O' GUINNESS
Fadó – 100 W. Grand Ave.
Celtic Crossings – 751 N. Clark St.
Irish Oak – 3511 N. Clark St.

TRIVIA   What *Cheers* regular frequently calls upon
Abbey Pub while in town?

NOTES   _____

_____

_____

_____

_____

_____

ANDY'S JAZZ CLUB

11 E. Hubbard Ave. (400N, 0W)
Chicago, IL 60611
(312) 642-6805

Website	www.andysjazzclub.com
Neighborhood	River North
Open 'til & Cover	1:30am (2am Sat, 1am Sun); $5–15
Drinks	Dirty martinis, domestic beer
Food	Reasonably priced pasta, steaks, fish
Music	Traditional, swing, and bebop jazz
Bar Type	Jazz Club, Cocktail Lounge

Named after its original owner, Andy's opened in 1951 and was a grungy hangout for *Chicago Tribune* and *Sun-Times* pressmen, much like nearby Billy Goat Tavern (p. 14). Scott Chisholm took over in 1974 and conducted an unlikely experiment four years later called *Jazz at Five*, which caught on and was followed up with the creatively named *Jazz at Noon* and *Jazz at Nine*. Andy's Jazz Club was born. While noontime jazz went the way of the three-martini lunch, some of Chicago's best live jazz is still featured here twice daily at 5pm and 9pm. Photos adorn the Wall of Fame across from the bar, highlighting internationally renowned performers who have played Andy's, such as Chicago's Franz Jackson, Wilbur Campbell, and Von Freeman (p. 138). Colorful banners hanging around the room commemorate the city's longest running lakefront music fest, the annual Chicago Jazz Festival held every Labor Day weekend. Jazz Fest is actually the culmination of three separate festivals: one memorializing Duke Ellington in 1974, one memorializing John Coltrane in 1978, and one planned by the Jazz Institute of Chicago's festival in 1978. The latter brought the first two together, marking Jazz Fest's official beginning, which Andy's has sponsored ever since. During the fest, tours between Andy's and many of the city's other jazz clubs are organized by the Jazz Institute of Chicago (www.jazz-inchicago.org).

NEARBY	Lucky Lady – 440 N. State St.
	Mother Hubbard's – 5 W. Hubbard St.
	Rossi's Liquors – 412 N. State St.
SIMILAR	**TOP JAZZ CLUBS**
	Jazz Showcase – 806 S. Plymouth Ct.
	BackRoom – 1007 N. Rush St.
	Green Mill Cocktail Lounge –
	4802 N. Broadway
	REINVENTED CHICAGO CLASSICS
	Marge's Still – 1758 N. Sedgwick (former dive)
	Mutiny – 2428 N. Western (former boxing bar)
	Fireside – 5739 N. Ravenswood (roadhouse)
TRIVIA	What new term was first used to describe music
	in 1915 by the *Chicago Daily Tribune*?
NOTES	_____
	_____
	_____
	_____
	_____
	_____

ANSWER: The word "jazz" itself.

BACKROOM

1007 N. Rush St. (1000N, 0E)
Chicago, IL 60611
(312) 751-2433

Website	www.backroomchicago.com
Neighborhood	Gold Coast
Open 'til & Cover	2am (3am Sat); $20–30 (half online)
Drinks	10 bottled beers, $10–12 cocktails
Food	Just the olive in your mini-martini
Music	Primarily jazz, also soul, funk, R&B
Bar Type	Jazz Club, Cocktail Lounge

BackRoom is one of the oldest jazz clubs in Chicago and the proverbial last man standing from the swingin' '60s Rush Street scene, once peppered with the likes of Mister Kelly's, London House, and the Playboy Club (p. 224). Top jazz is heard from Chicago's best vocalists, trios, and quartets, seven nights a week, starting around 9:15pm. BackRoom is located on Rush Street, just south of the "Viagra Triangle" (formed by Bellevue, State, and Rush), and adjacent to Jilly's (formerly Remington's and Gold Coast Lounge). Both clubs share the same address and building, though are unconnected inside. The BackRoom's entrance is an elaborately sculpted metal door flanked by two bouncers in suits like Chinese Foo Dogs guarding the entrance to a temple. The crowd predominantly consists of older Gold Coasters, middle-aged tourists, urban sugar daddies, those on an expense account, and the occasional B-list celebrity. BackRoom is a good spot to impress a date, especially after dinner at Gibson's, Morton's, or Carmine's, just to name a few of the best restaurants in the area. This is how it has always been at BackRoom since its opening in 1970. Before then, the place is reputed to have been a jazz club as far back as 1939, before which the building was used as a garage, and a horse stable prior to that.

NEARBY	Jilly's – 1007 N. Rush St
	Whiskey Bar & Grill – 1015 N. Rush St.
	Hugo's Frog Bar – 1024 N. Rush St.
SIMILAR	**TOP JAZZ CLUBS**
	Andy's Jazz Club – 11 E. Hubbard St.
	Jazz Showcase – 806 S. Plymouth Ct.
	Green Mill Cocktail Lounge – 4800 N. Broadway
	OTHER VIAGRA TRIANGLE FAVORITES
	Tavern on Rush – 1031 N. Rush St.
	Dublin's – 1030 N. State St.
	Blue Agave Bar & Grill – 11 W. Maple St.
TRIVIA	Located a little further south, which Chicago club, with a name that invokes the feeling, is also accessible via a narrow, brick-lined portal?
NOTES	_____
	_____
	_____
	_____
	_____
	_____

ANSWER: *Le Passage.*

BEACHWOOD INN

1415 N. Wood St. (1400N, 1800W)
Chicago, IL 60622
(773) 486-9806

Website	None
Neighborhood	Wicker Park
Open 'til & Cover	2am (3am Sat); never a cover
Drinks	Cheep bottled beer and booze
Food	None – Order your own pizza in
Music	Jukebox stocked with varied 80s tunes
Bar Type	Neighborhood Tavern, Dive Bar

The Beachwood Inn is one of Wicker Park's lesser-known taverns, but a diamond in the rough for neighborhood locals and historic tavern enthusiasts alike. Beachwood opened in 1950 by Leonard Stepien and takes its name from its location at the northeast corner of Beach Avenue and Wood Street. Stepien was shot and killed by an armed robber in the early 1960s and his spirit is said to haunt the place today. Stepien's wife, Lorraine, took over after his death and was mentored by the legendary neighborhood pub owner, transvestite, and bookmaker, Lottie Zagorski herself (himself). Lottie's is still located a few blocks north (p. 114). Sons Jim and Bob Stepien eventually took over running the family venture, the latter of whom was also shot by an unruly patron, but it was in the arm and not life-threatening. What may be mistaken for a sports bar from its exterior sign and neon homage to Chicago sports is actually a classic Wicker Park corner bar with the usual scruffsters as its main clientele. This new crowd and wave of gentrification chased off the ruffians and blue-collar crowd that once had to be buzzed in to enter. The Beachwood Inn is very chill and popular, with a stash of boardgames, a pool table, pinball machines, and eclectic décor featuring Old Style beer memorabilia, an old wooden phone booth (sans phone), and an impressive array of old movie posters, including *Clockwork Orange* and *Bloodsucking Freaks*.

NEARBY	Davenport's – 1383 N. Milwaukee Ave.
	Double Door – 1572 N. Milwaukee Ave.
	Lottie's Pub – 1925 W. Cortland St.
SIMILAR	**LESSER-KNOWN BOHEMIAN ALE HOUSES**
	Weeds Tavern – 1555 N. Dayton St.
	Hungry Brain – 2319 W. Belmont Ave.
	Ten Cat – 3931 N. Ashland Ave.
	NEAR WEST SIDE ORIGINALS
	Chipp Inn – 832 N. Greenview Ave.
	Lincoln Tavern – 1858 W. Wabansia Ave.
	Inner Town Pub – 1935 W. Thomas St.
TRIVIA	What other historic Chicago corner pub is named for the two streets upon which it is located?

NOTES

_____

_____

_____

_____

_____

_____

BEAUMONT

2020 N. Halsted St. (2000N, 800W)
Chicago, IL 60614
(773) 281-0177

Website	www.beaumontchicago.com
Neighborhood	Lincoln Park
Open 'til & Cover	3am (4am Sat); $5–10 Thu–Sat late
Drinks	Cheap domestics on tap, in beer tubs
Food	Standard pub grub, Saturday brunch
Music	Decent wall-mounted jukebox
Bar Type	Meat Market, Late-Night, Sports Bar

Beaumont is the Dr. Jekyll and Mr. Hyde of the North Side bar scene—by day, a dimly lit, low-key Chicago classic, by night a Bacchanalian spring break dance party. It's been this way since Beaumont opened in 1980. Step through the door and you'll find that signature Chi-town barroom setup: a long wooden bar, antique light fixtures, and a tin ceiling. Beaumont serves an all-you-can-eat brunch on Saturday, à la nearby Stanley's (1970 N. Lincoln), but is oddly closed on Sunday presumably due to the staff's atonement of the previous night's sins in confessional booths at nearby St. Vincent de Paul. Around midnight, the rear doors—almost unnoticeable during the day—open to reveal a warehouse-like space where a mostly 20s crowd flies in like stink on a monkey. An elevated stage features Lincoln Park's version of *Girls Gone Wild*, dancing to a Bud Light–soaked crowd doing the group-grope to a cheeseball mix that sounds like the greatest hits of B96. Beware: They often usher you out a half-hour early without announcing last call. Beaumont is the kind of place that attracts debauchery, adolescent behavior, and excessive intoxication—and that's just when the Hash House Harriers stop by on a school night...

NEARBY   Marquee Lounge – 1973 N. Halsted St.
Kincade's – 950 W. Armitage Ave.
Black Duck Tavern & Grille –
1800 N. Halsted St.

SIMILAR   **LINCOLN PARK CLASSICS-COME-PARTY CENTRAL**
John Barleycorn Memorial Pub –
658 W. Belden Ave.
Glascott's Groggery – 2158 N. Halsted St.
Burwood Tap – 724 W. Wrightwood Ave.
MORE 4AM LINCOLN PARK LECHERY
The Store – 2002 N. Halsted St.
Frank's – 2503 N. Clark St.
Rockhouse – 2624 N. Lincoln Ave.

TRIVIA   Who are the Hash House Harriers?

NOTES   _____

_____

_____

_____

ANSWER: *An international syndicate of drinkers with a running problem whose Chicago chapter infamously caused the 2007 anthrax scare at Lincoln Park Zoo by marking their running trail with small piles of white flour.*

BILLY GOAT TAVERN

430 N. Lower Michigan Ave. (430N, 100E)
Chicago, IL 60611
(312) 222-1525

Website	www.billygoattavern.com
Neighborhood	Magnificent Mile (beneath, that is)
Open 'til & Cover	7am–2am Mon–Fri, 10am–3am Sat,
	11am–2 am Sun; never a cover
Drinks	Billy Goat "Light" & "Dark" on tap
Food	"Doublecheez! *Triple* for the big guy!"
Music	Just chitter-chatter of the regs, tourists
Bar Type	Neighborhood Tavern (sans 'hood)

What appears to be a dive is a celebrated tavern that has gained more infamy since Prohibition than any other Chicago bar. Intriguingly located on an underground corner, the Billy Goat Tavern is the second location for founder and Greek immigrant William "Billy Goat" Sianis. Billy Goat assumed his name after adopting a goat that fell off a truck and wandered into his original joint, Lincoln Tavern, once located across from the Chicago Stadium (now United Center). Known for publicity stunts, Billy Goat brought his goat into Wrigley Field for the 1945 World Series but was kicked out by owner Philip K. Wrigley. Sianis famously cursed: "The Cubs, they not gonna win anymore!" The Cubs lost the series and haven't been back. Sianis opened the Billy Goat Tavern at its current location in 1964. A decade later, it was immortalized by locals Don Novello, John Belushi, and Bill Murray in a *Saturday Night Live* sketch inspired by current owner Sam Sianis, Billy Goat's nephew, and the Greek staff with their penchant for dictating your order: "Doublecheez! No fries, CHEEPS! No Pepsi, COKE!" Though a tourist trap today, the *Chicago Tribune* and *Sun-Times* are located a stairwell above at ground level, and the Billy Goat has famously attracted pressmen and journalists alike, including Pulitzer Prize winning columnist, Mike Royko, and a even few U.S. presidents. Today's columnists Rick Kogan and John Kass still drop by for a beer with the common man.

NEARBY	Mother Hubbard's – 5 W. Hubbard St.
	Andy's Jazz Club – 11 E. Hubbard St.
	Rock Bottom Brewery – 1 W. Grand Ave.
SIMILAR	**MORE CHICAGO LEGENDS**
	Butch McGuire's – 20 W. Division St.
	17 West at the Berghoff – 17 W. Adams St.
	Green Mill Cocktail Lounge –
	4802 N. Broadway
	CELEBRITY JOINTS
	Miller's Pub – 134 S. Wabash Ave.
	Old Town Ale House – 219 W. North Ave.
	Twin Anchors – 1655 N. Sedgwick St.
TRIVIA	What was the name of the original billy goat?

NOTES

_____

_____

_____

_____

_____

_____

B.L.U.E.S.

2519 N. Halsted St. (2500N, 800W)
Chicago, IL 60614
(773) 528-1012

Website	www.chicagobluesbar.com
Neighborhood	Lincoln Park
Open 'til & Cover	2am (3am Sat); $8–10 cover
Drinks	Domestic bottled beer, cocktails
Food	None (not even pretzels)
Music	It's just blues. Period.
Bar Type	Blues Club

Of all the blues clubs in Chicago, B.L.U.E.S. has survived the longest at its original location—even longer than the annual Chicago Blues Festival has been held. Rob Hecko and Bill Gillmore opened B.L.U.E.S. in April 1979, after purchasing the bar formerly called Omni. The idea for a blues bar came from Gillmore, who had booked bands for years. Since then, B.L.U.E.S. has featured its namesake music every night, seven days a week, 365 days a year. Kingston Mines, now much larger, moved in across the street in February 1982, which had B.L.U.E.S. owners nervous until their revenues tripled and the North Side's "Blues Alley" was born. Notable B.L.U.E.S. musicians include Sunnyland Slim, Big Time Sarah, and Eddy Clearwater, some of whom drop by in-between sets at Kingston Mines. There isn't much room to dance, but if you're in the mood to shake a tailfeather, no one will stop you. The popularity of B.L.U.E.S. stems from its maintaining a balance between authenticity, local appeal, and international notoriety. A second location, called B.L.U.E.S. Etcetera, opened on Belmont Avenue in 1987 and lasted until 1999. Tuesday night is "good neighbor night," when locals get in for free with an address on their driver's license displaying zip code 60610, 60614, or 60657. Others have to pay full price, but are likely to get discounts on future admissions upon departure.

NEARBY	Kingston Mines – 2548 N. Halsted St.
	Burwood Tap – 724 W. Wrightwood Ave.
	Victory Liquors – 2610 N. Halsted St.
SIMILAR	**BLUES CLUBS, FARTHER AFIELD**
	Rosa's Lounge – 3420 W. Armitage Ave.
	Buddy Guy's Legends – 754 S. Wabash Ave.
	New Checkerboard Lounge –
	5201 S. Harper Ct.
	COZY NEIGHBORHOOD MUSIC CLUBS
	Green Mill Cocktail Lounge –
	4802 N. Broadway
	Elbo Room – 2871 N. Lincoln Ave.
	Subterranean – 2011 W. North Ave.
TRIVIA	What legendary blues film was shot in Chicago?
NOTES	_____
	_____
	_____
	_____
	_____
	_____

BREHON PUB

731 N. Wells St. (800N, 200W)
Chicago, IL 60610
(312) 642-1071

Website	www.brehonpub.com
Neighborhood	River North
Open 'til & Cover	2am (3am Sat); never a cover
Drinks	17 beers and Jägermeister on tap
Food	Americanized pub grub, shepherd's pie
Music	Good jukebox, bagpipes for St. Patty's
Bar Type	Neighborhood Tavern, Irish Pub

The building housing Brehon Pub dates back to shortly after the Great Chicago Fire of 1871. Since then, the first floor has served as the United Linen Supply in the 1950s and the Firehouse Restaurant in the 1970s, just prior to its being leased from August through October of 1977 to the *Chicago Sun-Times*—yes, the *Sun-Times*—who opened the space as the "Mirage Tavern." Why did one of the city's major newspapers open a bar? Old-fashioned, investigative journalism. In this case, the targets were corrupt city inspectors taking bribes. Reporters Pam Zekman and Zay Smith from the *Sun-Time*s, together with the Better Government Association, hired photographer Jim Frost to document inspectors taking up to $100 kickbacks for overlooking health and safety code violations, and state liquor inspectors involved in a tax-skimming scheme. Frost took these photos while hidden at the back of the room, on an elevated platform over the men's can. The sting led to 34 convictions, Mike Wallace featured the story on *60 Minutes*, and Zekman and Smith nearly won a Pulitzer Prize. The building then lay vacant until 1980, when the Brothers Burke opened the Brehon Pub. The Burkes are of Irish ancestry and named their bar after a medieval form of Irish civil law, referenced in their family's coat of arms along with the motto "Ung Roy, Ung Foy, Ung Loy," meaning "One King, One Faith, One Law." Brehon Pub is a relaxed neighborhood hangout and a good place for darts.

NEARBY	Blue Frog Bar & Grill – 676 N. LaSalle Dr.
	Clark Street Ale House – 742 N. Clark St.
	Celtic Crossings – 751 N. Clark St.
SIMILAR	**RIVER NORTH FAUX IRISH**
	O'Leary's Public House – 541 N. Wells St.
	The Kerryman – 661 N. Clark St.
	Shamrock Club – 210 W. Kinzie St.
	LAWYER SALOONS
	Monk's Pub – 205 W. Lake St.
	Mother Hubbard's – 5 W. Hubbard St.
	Emmit's Pub – 495 N. Milwaukee Ave.
TRIVIA	What does "Brehon" mean in Gaelic?

NOTES

_____

_____

_____

_____

_____

_____

_____

_____

ANSWER: Judge.

BUDDY GUY'S LEGENDS

754 S. Wabash Ave. (800S, 100E)
Chicago, IL 60605
(312) 427-0333

Website	www.buddyguys.com
Neighborhood	South Loop
Open 'til & Cover	2am (3am Fri/Sat); $10–15 cover
Drinks	Standard beer and booze
Food	Cajun: jambalaya, gumbo, po' boys
Music	Top-shelf blues, with Buddy sometimes
Bar Type	Blues Club

The son of a Louisiana sharecropper, legendary bluesman and Rock & Roll Hall of Fame inductee George "Buddy" Guy first arrived in Chicago in 1957, penniless and hungry, but he impressed Muddy Waters and started playing in his band. In the 1970s, Buddy kept his '58 Stratocaster behind the bar at his own club, the Checkerboard Lounge (p. 140), to challenge ambitious patrons. Many lean years later, Guy opened his current club in 1989 in the 1910 South Loop building owned by Columbia College, just prior to his breakout *24 Nights* tour with Eric Clapton. Legends today features top-notch blues, though Buddy Guy himself only plays in January as part of his annual, month-long tenure. Like Guy's former club, Legends has kept true to its name by hosting the Rolling Stones, Eric Clapton, and Koko Taylor. The crowd consists mainly of tourists, suburbanites, and blues aficionados. In January 2007, Buddy Guy announced his club would close due to Columbia College's plan to build a student center but the school relented. As with the Checkerboard before, the club is part of a promise made to the late Muddy Waters to keep the blues alive on Chicago's South Side. Legends is also a must-visit during the annual Chicago Blues Festival every June… you just might find Buddy Guy himself sitting at the end of the bar, sipping the beloved cognac that he calls "Connie."

NEARBY
: Kitty O'Shea's – 720 S. Michigan Ave. (Hilton)
South Loop Club – 701 S. State St.
Jazz Showcase – 806 S. Plymouth Ct.

SIMILAR
: **SOUTH SIDE BLUES**
New Checkerboard Lounge –
    5201 S. Harper Ct.
Lee's Unleaded Blues – 7401 S. South Chicago
Linda's Place – 1044 W. 51st St.
NORTH SIDE BLUES
B.L.U.E.S. – 2519 N. Halsted St.
Kingston Mines – 2548 N. Halsted St.
Rosa's Lounge – 3420 W. Armitage Ave.

TRIVIA
: What famous guitarist, first inspired by seeing Buddy Guy in 1965, calls Guy the "pilot" to the course of his epic career?

NOTES

_____

_____

_____

_____

_____

_____

ANSWER: *Eric Clapton.*

BURWOOD TAP

724 W. Wrightwood Ave. (2600N, 700W)
Chicago, IL 60614
(773) 525-2593

Website	www.burwoodtap.com
Neighborhood	Lincoln Park
Open 'til & Cover	2am (3am Sat); never a cover
Drinks	Good selection on tap
Food	Limited pub grub, happy hour buffets
Music	Cheeseball jukebox
Bar Type	Neighborhood Tavern, Sports Bar

Tucked into the quiet hollows of the Wrightwood Neighbors enclave of Lincoln Park, at the corner of Burling and Wrightwood, lies the Burwood Tap. Its candy-striped awning is a nod to its Prohibition phase when a soda shop fronted the speakeasy in back. Once the "Noble Experiment" ended in 1933, Burwood Tap was founded with one of the city's first 20 liquor licenses, behind Berghoff (p. 2) and Coq d'Or (p. 38). Leading the third generation of family ownership, Albert Rompza remodeled the joint in the 1980s from an old man's pub into a lively destination for an increasingly younger neighborhood crowd. Beer tubs and all-you-can-drink specials in the back room are common on weekends, as are happy hour buffets on weekdays. The stately wooden bar, ancient cash register, and old-fashioned light fixtures are almost lost amidst a cacophony of sporting memorabilia, beer signage, and such random elements as a strap from an old Halsted streetcar. A pool table hogs most of the space on the landing separating the front room from the rear, and there you'll also find a vintage photograph of "The 'Wood." In addition to winning several annual "Best Neighborhood Bar" accolades, the Burwood Tap received a special commendation by the City of Chicago for providing aid and comfort to those affected by the nearby apartment porch collapse in 2003 that resulted in 12 deaths.

NEARBY   Kingston Mines – 2458 N. Halsted St.
Victory Liquors – 2610 N. Halsted St.
aliveOne – 2683 N. Halsted St.

SIMILAR   **LINCOLN PARK CLASSICS–COME–PARTY CENTRAL**
John Barleycorn Memorial Pub –
658 W. Belden Ave.
Glascott's Groggery – 2158 N. Halsted St.
Beaumont – 2020 N. Halsted St.
BEVY OF BAR-O-BELIA
Green Door Tavern – 678 N. Orleans St.
Hangge Uppe – 14 W. Elm St.
Chicago Joe's – 2256 W. Irving Park Rd.

TRIVIA   What Burwood Tap regular did Jim Croce sing about?

NOTES   _____

_____

_____

_____

_____

ANSWER: "Bad, bad, Leroy Brown," who was allegedly rather nice and a hell of a pool player.

BUTCH MCGUIRE'S

20 W. Division St. (1200N, 0W)
Chicago, IL 60610
(312) 337-9080

Website	www.butchmcguires.com
Neighborhood	Gold Coast
Open 'til & Cover	3am (4am Sat); never a cover
Drinks	Domestics & cocktails served in steins
Food	Pub grub & full w/e brunch until 4pm
Music	Jukebox with classic rock, blues
Bar Type	Neighborhood Tavern, Irish Pub

Before it housed Butch McGuire's, this building functioned as a speakeasy called Kelly's Pleasure Palace during Prohibition, and a strip club known as Bobby Farrell's Sho Lounge in the '50s. Robert "Butch" McGuire opened up the "mother of all singles bars" in 1961 with a $560 loan from his mother. McGuire was one of the first to serve Guinness and Harp on tap, and the first reputable bar owner to welcome unescorted women—unusual for the time. McGuire even rehabbed the women's "powder room" to make it one of the cleanest in the city, allowed only women to sit at the bar when crowded (men would give up their seat or be thrown out), and was one of the first to hire a female bartender. As such, Butch McGuire's claims responsibility for over 6,500 marriages. In its early days, even Hugh Hefner of *Playboy* would swing by, as would John Wayne when in town, who liked to repay the kindness of those who bought him a drink with a hearty, "Now f*** off!" Though Butch passed on in 2006, his legacy lives on as "the standard by which all other Division Street bars are judged." Be sure to check out the impressive decorations adorning Butch McGuire's every St. Patty's Day and Christmas, including a model train that runs around the bar, as well as the Waterford crystal in the west room from Butch's personal collection.

NEARBY	Mother's, The Original – 26 W. Division St.
	The Lodge – 21 W. Division St.
	She-nannigan's House of Beer – 16 W. Division
SIMILAR	**CLASSIC SINGLES BARS**
	Durkin's – 810 W. Diversey Pkwy.
	Burwood Tap – 724 W. Wrightwood Ave.
	Excalibur Nightclub – 632 N. Dearborn St.
	IRISH-TINGED NEIGHBORHOOD CLASSICS
	Schaller's Pump – 3714 S. Halsted St.
	Cork & Kerry – 10614 S. Western Ave.
	Kelly's Pub – 949 W. Webster Ave.
TRIVIA	Though McGuire's claims to have served the first celery stalk with a Bloody Mary, where did this actually occur?

NOTES _____

_____

_____

_____

_____

_____

ANSWER: *The nearby Pump Room, when a customer grabbed a celery stalk from a nearby garnish tray.*

CALIFORNIA CLIPPER

1002 N. California Ave. (1000N, 2800W)
Chicago, IL 60622
(773) 384-CLIP

Website	www.californiaclipper.com
Neighborhood	Humboldt Park
Open 'til & Cover	2am (3am Sat); never a cover
Drinks	Classic cocktails, like Purple Martin
Food	Only if you brought your own Cheetos
Music	Live weekend rockabilly and blues
Bar Type	Neighborhood, Music Venue, Haunted

What is now a classic Chicago tavern was a movie house from 1912 to 1918, which was closed to protect the public during the Spanish Flu epidemic that broke out during World War I. The space re-opened in 1937 as the Clipper Tavern by the Caporusso family until the place was sold, renovated, and re-opened in 1999 as the California Clipper. Named for both the tavern's address and the 1930s Boeing B314 "flying palace" seaplane, the California Clipper opened at a time when Humboldt Park was just starting to gentrify after years of domination by gangs and poverty, and quickly became a hotspot for West Side bohemians and adventurous North Siders. With a nod to its past, the Clipper features 1940s-era décor and an original Brunswick bar. Red leather booths line the opposite wall and feature vintage vacation posters, framed in what looks like ornate brass but is really gutters that were cut, drilled, and painted by the one-time upstairs resident, Frank Zych. Another Clipper regular is the apparition of a woman in white seen lounging in booths one and nine and who leaves a perfume cloud in front of the bar and restroom after hours. The Clipper also hosts some of the city's best rockabilly on weekends, bingo on Monday night (with a "bag of crap" as the main prize), and literary events organized by the Literary Guild Complex. Though rarely open to the public, the back room is festooned in tiki décor.

NEARBY	Continental – 2801 W. Chicago Ave.
	The Beetle – 2532 W. Chicago Ave.
	Blind Robin – 853 N. Western Ave.
SIMILAR	**REVELING IN BYGONE ERAS**
	Rainbo Club – 1150 N. Damen Ave.
	Marie's Riptide Lounge –
	1750 W. Armitage Ave.
	Zebra Lounge – 1220 N. State Pkwy.
	CHICAGO ROCKABILLY JOINTS
	Abbey Pub – 3420 W. Grace St.
	Hideout – 1354 W. Wabansia Ave.
	Schubas Tavern – 3159 N. Southport Ave.
TRIVIA	What Pultizer Prize–winning Chicago novelist from Humboldt Park had a bootlegger father?
NOTES	_____
	_____
	_____
	_____
	_____
	_____

ANSWER: Saul Bellow.

CAROL'S PUB

4659 N. Clark St. (4700N, 1500W)
Chicago, IL 60640
(773) 334-2402

Website	None
Neighborhood	Uptown
Open 'til & Cover	3am (4am Sat); $5 weekend cover
Drinks	Cheap domestics with pitcher specials
Food	Burgers, pizza puffs, fries
Music	Both kinds: country *and* western
Bar Type	Country Bar, Dive Bar, Late-Night

When my mother, who grew up in Humboldt Park, used to complain about all the, "hillbillies hangin' out the windows," in Lakeview and Uptown, I thought she was crazy. She was right: It turns out that there was indeed a wave of Appalachian migration that descended upon Chicago around the time Carol's Pub opened in 1973. This influence has largely passed, but Carol's Pub hangs on thanks to owner Carol Harris, who took over for her husband who moved on to the Big Honky Tonk in the Sky in 1993. The joint's kitschy charms include country on the jukebox, karaoke on Thursday nights, and the resident band Diamondback, which plays about seven sets of old-school country covers—Willie Nelson, Hank Williams, Johnny Cash, and more—until the wee hours every Friday and Saturday, just as they've done for over a decade. A quiet, local crowd drinks cheap domestic beer at the battered wooden bar and plays pinball, darts, and pool until the younger Wrigleyville and Loyola University hordes pack the place after other bars close, some wearing cowboy boots and hats. Grizzled regulars scope out the incoming talent and spin the girls on the dance floor, which is its own source of entertainment. With Adam Smith's invisible hand reaching in, drink prices escalate with increasing demand past midnight, so order your pitchers prior to the witching hour and, as the signs urge, remember to leave quietly!

NEARBY	Max's Place – 4621 N. Clark St.
	Green Mill Cocktail Lounge –
	4800 N. Broadway
	Uptown Lounge – 1136 W. Lawrence Ave.
SIMILAR	**COUNTRY MUSIC BARS**
	Montrose Saloon – 2933 W. Montrose Ave.
	Horseshoe – 4115 N. Lincoln Ave.
	Joe's Sports Bar – 940 W. Weed St.
	FAR NORTH LATE-NIGHT SCENES
	Fireside Lounge – 5739 N. Ravenswood Ave.
	Hidden Cove – 5336 N. Lincoln Ave.
	Mark II Lounge – 7436 N. Western Ave.
TRIVIA	What's the name of the honky tonk in the film, *The Blues Brothers*?

NOTES

_____

_____

_____

_____

_____

_____

ANSWER: Ray's Country Bunker.

CHICAGO BRAUHAUS

4732 N. Lincoln Ave. (4800N, 2400W)
Chicago, IL 60625
(773) 784-4444

Website	www.chicagobrauhaus.com
Neighborhood	Lincoln Square
Open 'til & Cover	2am (closed Tue); never a cover
Drinks	German beer, from stein to 64-oz. boot
Food	Wienerschnitzel, sausage, and the like
Music	Daily oompah & oompah-fied pop
Bar Type	German Restaurant, Beer Hall

In 1963, Harry Kempf immigrated from Germany and labored as a tool and die worker. After dreaming of a place where he could play live music every night, Harry opened Zum Lieben Augustin at 4560 N. Lincoln (now Daily Bar & Grill). Once his brother Guenther arrived two years later, the pair opened Treffpunkt (German for "meeting") across from their present location—a hit for years and visited by Ronald Reagan. The Kempf Brothers then began the neighborhood's Oktoberfest in 1979 (actually called German-American Fest) to draw more business after traffic was re-routed around Lincoln Avenue to make the heart of Lincoln Square more pedestrian-friendly. A 1984 fire wiped out the entire block where Treffpunkt was located, so the Kempf Brothers moved to their present location, once a bowling alley, Roehrich's Furniture, and then a catering operation that the Kempfs had wisely bought a few years earlier. As Germans kept fleeing the neighborhood, the new place was named "Chicago Brauhaus" to broaden its appeal. Today, the Brauhaus attracts neighborhood residents, tourists, and suburban teens learning the German language, just as I did in middle school. Young and old alike also love Gody Windischhofer, the "Austrian Elvis," who entertains the crowd with his oompah band and "sausage relays." During Oktoberfest, watch for the tuba player who walks around receiving quarter tips thrown into his tuba as he plays.

NEARBY	Huettenbar – 4721 N. Lincoln Ave.
	Hansa Clipper – 4659 N. Lincoln Ave.
	Resi's Bierstube – 2034 W. Irving Park Rd.
SIMILAR	**MORE GERMANIC RESTAURANTS & TAVERNS**
	Laschet's Inn – 2119 W. Irving Park Rd.
	Mirabell – 3454 W. Addison St. (Austrian)
	Lutz Continental Café –
	2458 W. Montrose Ave.
	THE NEW BREED OF GERMAN BARS
	Glunz Bavarian Haus – 4128 N. Lincoln Ave.
	Überstein – 3478 N. Clark St.
	17 West at the Berghoff – 17 W. Adams St.
TRIVIA	What is the right way to hold a beer stein & why?
NOTES	_____
	_____
	_____
	_____
	_____
	_____

ANSWER: Fingers through the handle with palm on glass to avoid bloody knuckles in a loud "Prost!"

CLUB LAGO

331 W. Superior St. (350W, 750N)
Chicago, IL 60610
(312) 337-9444

Website	www.clublago.com
Neighborhood	River North
Open 'til & Cover	10pm (11pm Fri/Sat, closed Sun); no $
Drinks	Bourbon, Chianti, Italian beer
Food	Reasonably priced Tuscan specialties
Music	Steel on ceramic with patron chatter
Bar Type	Neighborhood Tavern, Italian Joint

Club Lago defines *old-school* and is like stepping back into 1952, when Gus and Ida Lazzerini purchased the joint from Charles Giometti. After emigrating from Lucca, Italy, the couple's intent was to provide *cucina Toscana* to the printers and paper salesmen who loved three-martini lunches and worked in what then was called Smoky Hollow because of the heavy air pollution from factories that moved in once railroad tracks were laid along the Chicago River's North bank. As artists and hip businesses later took over the old loft buildings, the area was transformed into *River North* and, in 1980, the Lazzerinis' son-in-law Francesco Nardini took over just as Italian food became more popular and wine replaced martinis. Nardini's sons, GianCarlo and Guido, now run Club Lago for the professional crowd at lunch and after work. Now that most of the Cabrini Green housing projects have been torn down, evenings and weekends are filled with new condo dwellers that have filled the vacuum. *Lago* means "lake" in Italian and the tavern sports a semi-nautical theme, accented with old photos of the tavern's history as well as drawings by the famous Chicago cartoonist, Don Chisolm. You won't lack for neighborhood feel: The Nardinis note, "We'll talk theater before a show, sports before a game, and politics before the revolution." After a chimney collapse in the adjacent building that destroyed the kitchen, Club Lago re-opened after a lengthy remodeling and has never been better.

NEARBY Nacional 27 – 325 W. Huron St.
Martini Ranch – 311 W. Chicago Ave.
Green Door Tavern – 678 N. Orleans St.

SIMILAR **OLD-SCHOOL TAVERN NOSH**
17 West at the Berghoff – 17 W. Adams St.
Club Lucky – 1824 W. Wabansia Ave.
Lincoln Tavern – 1858 W. Wabansia Ave.
NAUTICALLY THEMED PUBS
Cove Lounge – 1750 E. 55th St.
Twin Anchors – 1655 N. Sedgwick St.
Simon's Tavern – 5210 N. Clark St.

TRIVIA What Bill Murray and Robert DeNiro film was shot at Club Lago?

NOTES _____

_____

_____

_____

_____

_____

_____

ANSWER: Mad Dog & Glory (1991).

CLUB LUCKY

1824 W. Wabansia Ave. (1700N, 1800W)
Chicago, IL 60622
(773) 227-2300

Website	www.clubluckychicago.com
Neighborhood	Bucktown
Open 'til & Cover	2am (3am Sat, 10pm Sun); no cover
Drinks	21 vodkas for martinis, shaken
Food	Authentic Sicilian and Southern Italian
Music	Rat Pack and Swing Band Jazz
Bar Type	Cocktail Lounge, Italian Joint

When Chicagoans think of top Italian dining, Rosebud, Italian Village, or Mia Francesca come to mind. When Chicagoans think of swanky lounges, Violet Hour, Lumen, or Funky Buddha Lounge are sought-after destinations. Only the savvy know where to find both: Club Lucky combines 1940s lounging glamour with authentic Sicilian cooking. The result is a sophisticated and comfortable Bucktown enterprise—not bad for a venue that still serves as a polling place for the 35th Ward and once was a Polish banquet hall. During Prohibition, Club Lucky operated as a speakeasy with a hardware store front and signature gin martinis downstairs. Step through the door today and you'll be transported into the time following the Volstead Act, when martinis outsold Budweiser and Tony Gondek opened the original Club Lucky, inspiring the present incarnation. With its Naugahyde booths, Formica-topped bar, and recessed ceiling, the lounge at Club Lucky is an exact replica of the original as it appeared in 1938. Dinner is served in the bar area, but I suggest the dining room, located up a few stairs and to the right of the bar. This lively space is ideal for enjoying reasonably-priced bruschetta, filet oreganato, and cannoli—all of which are recommended. At Club Lucky you get the feeling that, at any moment, a black limousine will pull up carrying a powerful politician, Sicilian Mafioso, or a world-class entertainer with a blonde on each arm...or at least Vince Vaughn getting out of a cab.

NEARBY   Northside Café – 1635 N. Damen Ave.
               Chaise Lounge – 1840 W. North Ave.
               Aberdeen – 1856 W. North Ave.

SIMILAR   **NEIGHBORHOOD ITALIAN**
               Club Lago (River North) – 331 W. Superior St.
               Tufano's (Little Italy) – 1073 W. Vernon Park Pl.
               Italian Village (Loop) – 71 W. Monroe St.
               NEW-SCHOOL YET CLASSIC LOUNGES
               Fulton Lounge – 955 W. Fulton Market
               Paramount Room – 415 N. Milwaukee Ave.
               Bungalow Lounge – 1622 W. Belmont Ave.

TRIVIA   In what year did Club Lucky open?

NOTES   _____

               _____

               _____

               _____

               _____

               _____

               _____

               _____

ANSWER: 1990 by Bobby Paladino & Jim Higgins.

COOGAN'S RIVERSIDE SALOON

180 N. Wacker Dr. (200N, 400W)
Chicago, IL 60606
(312) 444-1134

Website	None
Neighborhood	Loop
Open 'til & Cover	10pm-ish (6pm Sat/Sun); never a cover
Drinks	Guinness & Harp, what else is needed?
Food	Primarily sandwiches under $7
Music	Chit-chat of colleagues
Bar Type	Irish Pub, After-Work

Being over 25 years old makes Coogan's one of the oldest pubs in Chicago's downtown Loop, named for the shape formed by all elevated "L" train lines as they loop the city's central business district. Coogan's is located in the Great Lakes Building, built as a mill in 1912. This was also the site of a temporary "wigwam" erected to hold thousands of delegates for the 1860 Republican National Convention and the nomination of Abraham Lincoln for President. Prior to that, the area was called "Wolf Point" and was the site of the Sauganash Tavern opened by Mark Beaubien in 1831. The Sauganash was Chicago's third tavern, behind Wolf Tavern (p. 220), and Miller House, and was named after Archibald "Billy" Caldwell, nicknamed "Sauganash" for "Englishman" in the Pottawatomi tongue. Though Beaubien apparently kept his tavern "like hell," it did host Chicago's first election (in 1833) and then a theater, but was destroyed by fire in 1851. The property was converted for office use in 1981 and Coogan's opened shortly thereafter. Today, the pub looks like a nineteenth-century saloon, with its tin ceiling, antique light fixtures, and an original 1898 Brunswick bar once used in an African saloon. The joint is very popular with the after-work crowd and those headed to the nearby Civic Opera House, built in 1929 by utility magnate Samuel Insull for his wife, thus inspiring the opera house featured in the film *Citizen Kane*.

NEARBY   Jimmy Fig's Tavern – 160 N. Franklin St.
Ghost Bar – 440 W. Randolph St.
Cardozo's Pub – 170 W. Washington St.

SIMILAR   **CLASSIC LOOP TAVERNS**
Monk's Pub – 205 W. Lake St.
Miller's Pub – 134 S. Wabash Ave.
Exchequer Pub – 226 S. Wabash Ave.
CHICAGO BARS ON THE WATER
Castaways – 1603 N. Lakeshore Dr.
Dick's Last Resort – 315 N. Dearborn St.
Flatwater – 321 N. Clark St.

TRIVIA   Who owned the city's fourth tavern, Green Tree Tavern?

NOTES   _____

_____

_____

_____

_____

_____

_____

ANSWER: *James Kinzie.*

Coq d'Or

140 E. Walton St. (1000N, 200E)
Chicago, IL 60611
(312) 787-2200

Website	www.thedrakehotel.com
Neighborhood	Gold Coast
Open 'til & Cover	2am (1am Sundays); never a cover
Drinks	16-ounce Martinis, wine, limited beer
Food	Limited; get the Bookbinder Soup
Music	Live piano jazz
Bar Type	Hotel Bar, Piano Lounge

At 8:30pm on December 6, 1933—the exact time our national tragedy of sobriety, lasting 14 years, was repealed in Illinois—Coq d'Or opened after obtaining the second liquor license from the City of Chicago, following The Berghoff (p. 2). What was it like? According to Coq d'Or: "The lines were so long that our bartenders only had time to pour whiskey at 40¢ a glass. Along with the rest of the city, we were ready, however, with an excess of 200,000 gallons of whiskey for the celebration that lasted until dawn." Coq d'Or is located in the lobby of the Drake Hotel (constructed in 1920), along with another Chicago classic, the Cape Cod Room restaurant. The clientele at Coq d'Or consists primarily of Drake Hotel guests and a few Gold Coast penthouse-dwellers, some of whom may be old enough to personally recall visits from past guests Winston Churchill, Emperor Hirohito, Queen Elizabeth II, Jawaharlal Nehru, Princess Diana, and Ronald Reagan. Coq d'Or, French for "golden cockerel" (a young rooster), is known for its nineteenth-century New England menu and décor, live piano jazz, and 16-ounce "Executive Martini." While many love the clam chowder, the Bookbinder Soup is even more delicious. Since 1967, this signature soup has been made with tomato stock and red snapper, and served with a petite carafe of sherry and an Asiago cheese roll. Yum.

NEARBY   Signature Lounge – 875 N. Michigan Ave., 96th Fl.

Seasons Bar – 120 E. Delaware Pl. (Four Seasons)

Le Passage – 937 N. Rush St.

SIMILAR   **CLASSIC HOTEL BARS**

Pump Room – 1301 N. State St. (Ambassador East)

Kitty O'Shea's – 720 S. Michigan Ave. (Hilton)

Lockwood – 17 E. Monroe St. (Palmer House)

NEAR NORTH PIANO LOUNGES

Redhead Piano Bar – 16 W. Ontario St.

Zebra Lounge – 1220 N. State St.

Underground Wonder Bar – 10 E. Walton St.

TRIVIA   What famous couple carved their initials on the bar in the Drake Hotel's Cape Cod Room?

NOTES   _____

_____

_____

_____

_____

_____

ANSWER: *Joe DiMaggio and Marilyn Monroe.*

CORK & KERRY

10614 S. Western Ave. (10600S, 2400W)
Chicago, IL 60643
(773) 445-2675

Website	www.corkandkerrychicago.com
Neighborhood	Beverly
Open 'til & Cover	2am (3am Sat); never a cover
Drinks	20 beers on tap, inc. Guinness & Harp
Food	All-you-can-eat free popcorn
Music	Decent, wall-mounted jukebox
Bar Type	Irish Pub, Neighborhood Tavern

An institution in the far South Side Irish neighborhood of Beverly since 1988, Cork & Kerry was named by the original owners Scott and Chad Weiler after two southwest counties in Ireland. Built in 1930 during Prohibition, there is a "silent pig" underneath the leafy and spacious beer garden where barrels were hidden during federal raids. Cork & Kerry was almost destroyed in a 1999 blaze, but re-opened in 2000 by Mount Carmel-ites, Mike Fitzgerald and Bill Guide. For the holidays, the pub strings up over 7,000 lights and several animatronic displays, à la Butch McGuire's (p. 24). Cork & Kerry was a top spot during the annual South Side Irish Parade (canceled after 2008), though they locked you in for an hour afterwards while local prisoners swept up post-parade detritus. Cork & Kerry is a also favorite on the "Western Walk," sometimes called the "Irish Death March"—a rite of passage requiring a beer at every bar on the west side of Western (the east side is dry), between Sean's Rhino Bar at 103rd and McNally's at 115th, though purists push it to Chandler's Lounge at 118th. Cork & Kerry also made an appearance in the movie *Chicago Overcoat* (2009) about the Chicago Outfit organized crime syndicate.

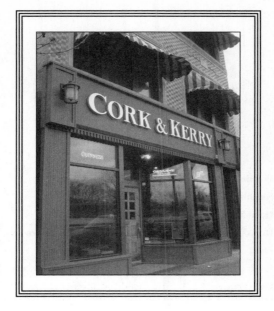

NEARBY   Keegan's Pub – 10618 S. Western Ave.
         Brewbakers – 10350 S. Western Ave.
         Dinger's Sports Bar – 10638 S. Western Ave.
SIMILAR MORE SOUTH SIDE IRISH
         Mrs. O'Leary's Dubliner –
            10910 S. Western Ave.
         Shamrock Express – 10934 S. Western Ave.
         McNally's – 11136 S. Western Ave.
         A MEAN PINT O' GUINNESS,
            NORTH SIDE–STYLE
         Fadó – 100 W. Grand Ave.
         Celtic Crossings – 751 N. Clark St.
         Irish Oak – 3511 N. Clark St.
TRIVIA   When did the South Side Irish Parade begin?

NOTES   _____

         _____

         _____

         _____

ANSWER: 1979 by George Hendry and Pat Coakley. It started
as a parade of children, and was later called The Wee
Folks of Washtenaw & Talman because of its route
around the block bordered by 109th, 110th,
Washtenaw, and Talman in Cajetan Parish.

COVE LOUNGE

1750 E. 55th St. (5500S, 1800E)
Chicago, IL 60615
(773) 684-1013

Website	None
Neighborhood	Hyde Park
Open 'til & Cover	2am (3am Sat), never a cover
Drinks	Four beers on tap, 28 in bottles
Food	A bag of nuts if you're lucky
Music	Internet jukebox (replaced 40s jazz)
Bar Type	Neighborhood Tavern, College Bar

Formerly "The 1750" and known for its frayed elegance, the Cove Lounge dates back to 1965 when they expanded into what once served as a socialist bookstore. The Art Deco marquee and a bar dating back to Prohibition gives the lounge the feel of stepping back in time, also reflected in the beer prices. Pitchers go for $6 on Thursday nights, attracting students and professors from nearby University of Chicago. A harpoon hangs over the back bar and, combined with the ship's wheel chandeliers and whale coathooks, completes the light nautical theme installed by former owner Dick O'Connell. Cove Lounge is cash-only but you'll find an ATM in the rear where, until recently, a local named "Speedy" once played jazz piano since as far back as 1967. It is said that Speedy's music inspired U of C grad school dropout Kurt Vonnegut to have written parts of his first novel, *Player Piano* (1952), here. Cove Lounge does not serve food so you may want to stop by Charlie's Pizza to the Falcon Inn on 53rd. Did Barack Obama ever drop by The Cove when he lived in Hyde Park and neighboring Kenwood? He probably wouldn't admit it even if he did, but yes, you can!

NEARBY   Bar Louie – 5500 S. Shore Dr.
Falcon Inn – 1601 East 53rd St.
New Checkerboard Lounge –
　　5201 S. Harper Ct.

SIMILAR   **CLASSIC DIVE BARS**
Weeds Tavern – 1555 N. Dayton St.
Rainbo Club – 1150 N. Damen Ave.
L&L Tavern – 3207 N. Clark St.
NAUTICALLY THEMED PUBS
Club Lago – 331 W. Superior St.
Twin Anchors – 1655 N. Sedgwick St.
Simon's Tavern – 5210 N. Clark St.

TRIVIA   What was the preferred greeting of Alexander
Graham Bell when answering the phone?

NOTES   _____

_____

_____

_____

_____

_____

ANSWER: Ahoy-hoy, which is how Mr. Burns of the Simpsons answers.

CUBBY BEAR

1059 W. Addison St. (3600N, 1100W)
Chicago, IL 60613
(773) 327-1662

Website	www.cubbybear.com
Neighborhood	Wrigleyville
Open 'til & Cover	2am (3am Sat); $5–10 cover at night
Drinks	$5 beer cans, cocktails in plastic cups
Food	Serviceable pub grub: wings & sangers
Music	A few big acts but mostly cover bands
Bar Type	Sports Bar, Music Venue

God knows it's hard to be a Cubs fan, but it's easy to like the Cubby Bear—a 30,000–square foot drunken paradise. We all know that the Chicago Cubs haven't won a World Series since 1908, but fans find solace in defeat and camaraderie in victory at the Cubby Bear, a Wrigleyville landmark since 1953. Previously known as Cubs Tap and Cubs Pub, Cubby Bear has weathered such storms as the pre-80s Appalachian Invasion (see Carol's Pub, p. 28), more lean years than any other team in the history of sports, and a massive influx of bars that has made Newport to Addison a wall-to-wall booze-fest. Today, Cubby Bear packs 'em in before and after Cub games (doors open as early as 10am), reinforcing the wisdom of "location, location, location"—Cubby Bear being opposite the main entrance and infamous marquee of Wrigley Field. In the off-season, the Cubby Bear draws a crowd by hosting cover bands like the Afrodisiacs (disco), Sixteen Candles (80s), and Elevation (U2), as well as occasional major acts that have included Violent Femmes, Flaming Lips, and Johnny Cash. Cubby Bear is owned by George and Patty Loukas, who run the adjacent Vines on Clark (expansive beer garden) and Cubby Bear North (Lincolnshire). The Cubby Café is located in the rear and is a good spot for watching Bears games and the NCAA basketball tournament. As a friend and Sox fan of mine likes to say: "Don't slip on the trail of tears on your way out…"

NEARBY   Goose Island Wrigleyville – 3535 N. Clark St.
John Barleycorn Wrigleyville – 3524 N. Clark St.
Red Ivy – 3525 N. Clark St.

SIMILAR   **CLASSIC WRIGLEYVILLE SPORTS BARS**
Yak-zies – 3710 N. Clark St.
Murphy's Bleachers – 3655 N. Sheffield Ave.
Sluggers – 3540 N. Clark St.
COVER BAND EMPORIUMS
Joe's Sports Bar – 940 W. Weed St.
McGee's – 950 W. Webster Ave.
McDunna's – 1505 W. Fullerton Ave.

TRIVIA   Who did the Cubs face in their last two World Series in 1908 and 1945?

NOTES   _____

_____

_____

_____

_____

_____

_____

ANSWER: The Detroit Tigers – won one, lost one...

CUNNEEN'S

1424 W. Devon Ave. (6400N, 1400W)
Chicago, IL 60660
(773) 274-9317

Website	None
Neighborhood	West Rogers Park
Open 'til & Cover	2am (3am Sat); never a cover
Drinks	Cheap domestics (cash only)
Food	Free peanuts; bags of chips & pretzels
Music	Oldies played on actual vinyl (and CD)
Bar Type	Neighborhood Tavern, Dive Bar

The low-key Cunneen's has become an institution in Rogers Park, an area once favored by the Pottawatomi and known for its ethnic diversity today. Inside, you'll find a narrow room with eclectic décor such as a less-than-politically-correct cigar store wooden Indian, two La-Z-Boy chairs, a Chicago flag, and black & white photos of the city's past. A neon-rimmed clock hangs above the bar with the face of original boss "Hizzoner" Mayor Richard J. Daley. A few thick wooden tables are found in the front windows overlooking Devon Avenue, often claimed by regulars playing *Scrabble*. Cheap beer and pitchers attract students and professors from nearby Loyola University as well as an older neighborhood clientele. Entertainment is provided by the 50¢ pool table, bartender-spun vinyl from their impressive collection (no jukebox), local news on the TVs, and selections from *The Onion* posted in the bathrooms. Cunneen's was named after the owner Steve Cunneen who opened the pub in 1974. The bar actually dates back to the end of Prohibition, from which commemorative articles can be found on the wall. If you're lucky, Bill Savage will be tending bar—a Northwestern University professor by day and brother of Dan Savage, known for his syndicated sex advice column, *Savage Love*.

NEARBY	Duke's Hideaway – 6920 N. Glenwood Ave.
	Pumping Company – 6157 N. Broadway
	Sovereign – 6202 N. Broadway
SIMILAR	**OTHER FAR NORTH CLASSICS**
	Heartland Café – 7000 N. Glenwood Ave.
	Hamilton's Pub – 6341 N. Broadway
	Candlelight Chicago – 7452 N. Western Ave.
	ALSO DIFFICULT TO SPELL
	Hangge Uppe – 14 W. Elm St.
	Jedynka Nightclub – 5610 W. Diversey (Polish)
	Poitin Stil – 1502 W. Jarvis Ave.
TRIVIA	What do the 4 stars on the Chicago flag stand for?

NOTES _____

_____

_____

_____

_____

_____

ANSWER: Fort Dearborn Massacre (1812), Great Chicago Fire (1871), World's Columbian Exposition (1893), and Century of Progress Exposition (1933).

DURKIN'S

810 W. Diversey Pkwy. (2800N, 800W)
Chicago, IL 60614
(773) 525-2515

Website	www.durkinstavern.com
Neighborhood	Lakeview
Open 'til & Cover	2am (3am Sat); never a cover
Drinks	Several imports/micros, daily specials
Food	Typical pub grub
Music	Top 40, played loudly
Bar Type	Neighborhood Tavern, Sports Bar

Though Durkin's holds the oldest continuous tavern license on the North Side, its history dates back even further, when a soda parlor operated in front and "Prohibition Willy's Speakeasy" raged on in back. Time had almost forgotten good ol' Willy until Margaret Durkin, who ran the joint since the Volstead Act was repealed in 1933, sold her namesake bar in 1974. During the ensuing renovation, workers discovered a basement full of bootlegged White Horse Scotch and Portuguese brandy (without government tax seals). Jerry Olson, of "no matter where you go, there you are" fame, then ran the bar for almost 30 years back when the Lakeview neighborhood was quite rough. Durkin's was dark and dingy with yellowed stucco walls until Bar 1 Events took over (they also own McGee's, Duffy's, Wrightwood Tap, and Redmond's). They cleaned up the place, aired it out with French windows, and even mounted a bronze statue at the end of the bar from the original Durkin's logo. Horseshoes, however, are no longer available in the adjacent alley. When the hunger pangs strike, Durkin's serves a selection of sandwiches, prepared by neighboring Select Cut Steakhouse (2808 N. Halsted) that includes one of the city's "Top 5" burgers according to *Chicago Tribune*. For entertainment, almost 40 televisions cater to a recently graduated Purdue University crowd and, of all things, Pittsburgh Steelers fans, so be sure to take note on game days.

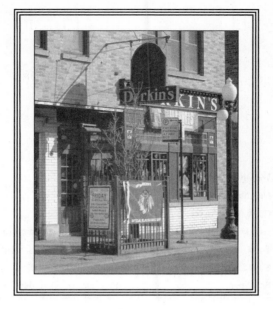

NEARBY	Harrigan's – 2816 N. Halsted St.
	Hidden Shamrock – 2723 N. Halsted St.
	Trinity – 2721 N. Halsted St.
SIMILAR	**NEW-SCHOOL NEIGHBORHOOD TAVERNS**
	Burwood Tap – 724 W. Wrightwood Ave.
	Glascott's Groggery– 2158 N. Halsted St.
	Schoolyard Tavern – 3258 N. Southport Ave.
	FAUX IRISH SPORTS BARS
	Schaller's Pump – 3714 S. Halsted St.
	Chicago Blarney Stone – 3424 N. Sheffield Ave.
	She-nannigan's House of Beer –
	16 W. Division St.
TRIVIA	When did Prohibition go into effect in the U.S.?
NOTES	_____
	_____
	_____
	_____
	_____
	_____

ANSWER: *January 16, 1920.*

EDGEWATER LOUNGE

5600 N. Ashland Ave. (5600N, 1400W)
Chicago, IL 60660
(773) 878-3343

Website	www.edgewaterlounge.com
Neighborhood	Andersonville
Open 'til & Cover	2am (3am Sat); never a cover
Drinks	15 craft brews on tap, more in bottles
Food	Homemade soups, sandwiches, salads
Music	Live Celtic and bluegrass on Tuesdays
Bar Type	Neighborhood Tavern, Dive Bar

"The Edgewater" has quenched Andersonville thirsts since 1970. The original owner, Mary, ran the joint for 25 years and then leased it to a man who ran it until he set the place on fire. The fire didn't take and the villain was never heard from again. Mary, who continued to live upstairs thereafter, has since passed on and allegedly haunts the floors above. The building dates back to 1901 and has been a tavern since 1908, serving as a speakeasy during Prohibition with an auto parts store serving as a front, booze in back, and poker downstairs. Current owner David Butler purchased the Edgewater Lounge, renovated it (except for its signature sun-bleached sign), and re-launched the pub in 2000, following the closure of both his short-lived Hop Cat Brewing Co. on Clybourn and the beloved Augenblick on Damen. Beer enthusiasts appreciate a connoisseur's array of craft beer on tap, including varieties seldom found elsewhere. Edgewater Lounge sells the most Rogue Ale in the Midwest, and David and his wife were even married at the Rogue Brewery in Oregon. The joint is also called upon by the filmmaking Wachowski Brothers (*Matrix*, *V for Vendetta*) when back in their hometown, perhaps before dropping in at Neo (p. 136) in Lincoln Park. After Edgewater Lounge, head over to nearby Ravenswood Pub for their Rock-Paper-Scissors tournament on Thursday nights, and Big Joe's 2 & 6 Pub for turtle racing on Friday nights.

NEARBY   Ravenswood Pub – 5455 N. Ravenswood Ave.
Big Joe's 2 & 6 Pub – 1818 W. Foster Ave.
Charlie's Ale House – 5308 N. Clark St.

SIMILAR   **OFF-THE-BEATEN-TRACK FORMER**
      SPEAKEASIES
Hideout – 1354 W. Wabansia Ave.
Inner Town Pub – 1935 W. Thomas St.
Emmit's Pub – 495 N. Milwaukee Ave.
REVIVED NEIGHBORHOOD CLASSICS
Kasey's Tavern – 701 S. Dearborn St.
Woodlawn Tap – 1172 E. 55th St.
Four Farthings Tavern – 2060 N. Cleveland Ave.

TRIVIA   What other filmmaking brothers like to drop in?

NOTES   _____

      _____

      _____

      _____

      _____

      _____

      _____

ELBO ROOM

2871 N. Lincoln Ave. (2900N, 1200W)
Chicago, IL 60657
(773) 549-5549

Website	www.elboroomchicago.com
Neighborhood	Lakeview
Open 'til & Cover	2am (3am Sat); $7–12
Drinks	50 beers available
Food	Upstairs bistro now for private parties
Music	Live alternative, rock, jazz, funk
Bar Type	Music Venue, Cocktail Lounge

What was originally conceptualized as a rotisserie restaurant turned into one of the best small alternative clubs in town. How did this happen? Located at the six-corner intersection of Lincoln, Lakeview, and George, Elbo Room takes its name from the elbow-like shape of the triangular building housing it, and the close proximity of tables in the original dining room. The space wound up being too small for a full-blown restaurant but big enough for a retro cocktail lounge, which it is now, creatively furnished with items found at local flea markets. The three-story brick building, once a factory set amongst meatpacking plants, includes a basement that is much bigger than the lounge. This provides enough space for performances, room to groove in front of the stage, a small bar, and seating around the room's perimeter. Bands begin at 9pm during the week and 10pm on Saturdays, and up to five play in one night. Since it opened in 1989 by Nick Henricks and David Friedman, Elbo Room has showcased many local and regional up-and-coming bands, including Liquid Soul, The Alarm, Smoking Popes, and Filter. With this legacy, and due to the closings of Lounge Ax, Morseland (resurrected as a restaurant), and Thurston's (once located across the street), Elbo Room is the city's oldest small venue for alternative music. Although Elbo Room once served food, the room above the cocktail lounge has been converted into a private party space – no rotisserie for you!

NEARBY	Vida Lounge – 1248 W. George St.
	Witt's – 2913 N. Lincoln Ave.
	Home Tavern – 2828 N. Lincoln Ave.
SIMILAR	**ROCKIN' SMALL CLUBS**
	Beat Kitchen – 2100 W. Belmont Ave.
	Empty Bottle – 1035 N. Western Ave.
	Underground Lounge – 952 W. Newport Ave.
	WHERE TO SEE THE NEXT BIG THING
	Metro – 3730 N. Clark St.
	Vic Theater – 3145 N. Sheffield Ave.
	Double Door – 1572 N. Milwaukee Ave.
TRIVIA	What 80s arcade game is found at Elbo Room?

NOTES

_____

_____

_____

_____

_____

_____

_____

_____

ANSWER: Ms. Pac-Man.

EXCALIBUR NIGHTCLUB

632 N. Dearborn St. (700N, 100W)
Chicago, IL 60610
(312) 266-1944

Website	www.excaliburchicago.com
Neighborhood	River North
Open 'til & Cover	4am (5am Sat), $10–20 (add'l upstairs)
Drinks	Cheesy test tube shots (1st floor)
Food	Average pub grub
Music	Retro downstairs, electronic upstairs
Bar Type	Nightclub, Cheeseball Palace, Haunted

Just hearing the name "Excalibur Nightclub" sends shivers down the spine of those who know it... *and* it's haunted. The enormous Gothic graystone known by Gold Coast locals as "the castle," dates back to 1892 when it served as the original Chicago Historical Society. Since then, the behemoth housed the Works Progress Administration, Institute of Design, *Gallery* magazine, and the Limelight nightclub. It received official landmark designation in 1997. Excalibur opened in 1989 and features 60,000-square feet of adult entertainment. The main floor features the retro Cabaret, drawing bachelorette parties like moths to the flame. The techno Club X is upstairs, overlooked by two balconies. The subterranean chamber is like a mini-Dave & Buster's and also features Neil Tobin's Supernatural Chicago show every Friday night—an interactive recounting of the hauntings at Excalibur. Ghosts range from those who perished in the former building during the Great Chicago Fire of 1871, to Jean LaLime, killed by Chicago's second permanent settler, John Kinzie. LaLime's bones were kept in the basement of the original Chicago Historical Society and thought to have burned in the fire, but were later unearthed by workmen. Excalibur also features an annual Halloween display that Jeffrey Dahmer would be proud of. Not bad for what many decry as a cheesy club version of Medieval Times, but without the Knights of the Roundtable schtick.

NEARBY	Vision Nightclub – 640 N. Dearborn St.
	Redhead Piano Bar – 16 W. Ontario St.
	Pops for Champagne – 601 N. State St.
SIMILAR	**CHEESEBALL DANCE CLUBS**
	Finn McCool's – 15 W. Division St. (same owner)
	She-nannigan's House of Beer –
	16 W. Division St.
	Beaumont – 2020 N. Halsted St. (also late-night)
	HAUNTED LEGENDS
	Hangge Uppe – 14 W. Division St.
	California Clipper – 1002 N. California Ave.
	Ole St. Andrew's Inn – 5938 N. Broadway
TRIVIA	Who once published *Gallery* magazine, after
	defending Dr. Sam Shepherd and Patty Hearst?

NOTES

_____

_____

_____

_____

_____

_____

ANSWER: F. Lee Bailey.

FIREPLACE INN

1448 N. Wells St. (1400N, 200W)
Chicago, IL 60610
(312) 943-7427

Website	www.fireplaceinn.com
Neighborhood	Old Town
Open 'til & Cover	2am (3am Sat); never a cover
Drinks	The usual & 32-oz vodka lemonades
Food	Ribs and steaks
Music	Nothing noticeable
Bar Type	Neighborhood Tavern, Rib Joint

The two-story brick building housing the Fireplace Inn goes back to 1873, erected just after the Great Conflagration of 1871. They don't call the neighborhood Old Town for nothing… Pre-dating the Fireplace Inn was a plumber, an insurance broker, a bookkeeper, and the short-lived Rigoletto Opera Café (1965). Two sales reps for a heavy equipment manufacturer, Dick and Jim Novak, then bought the place in 1969. There weren't many rib joints in town back then, so the Brothers Novak applied their culinary passion to their new business venture and the place has been known for its mouth-watering ribs ever since. Enjoy them at the restaurant or during the annual summertime culinary showdown and people-herding extravaganza, *Taste of Chicago*. Outdoor seating is available in either the sidewalk café or the canopied beer garden (retractable in summer and heated in winter), both of which are major people-watching outposts during the annual Wells Street Art Festival. Inside you'll find more cozy quarters, warmed by the namesake fireplace that stands opposite an impressive array of blacksmith tools. An enormous chandelier 8' in diameter and 6' long that was obtained from Chicago's old federal court building lights the room. With its popularity and proximity to downtown, the Fireplace Inn has attracted many celebrities through the years, including Tom Hanks, Liza Manelli, Cubs players, and anchors from local news outlets.

NEARBY   Burton Place – 1447 N. Wells St.
              O'Brien's Restaurant & Bar – 1528 N. Wells St.
              Old Town Ale House – 219 W. North Ave.
SIMILAR   **WARM FIREPLACES**
              Southport City Saloon – 2548 N. Southport Ave.
              Friar Tuck – 3010 N. Broadway
              Moody's Pub – 5910 N. Broadway
              RIB JOINT HIDEAWAYS
              Twin Anchors – 1655 N. Sedgwick St.
              Gale Street Inn – 4914 N. Milwaukee Ave.
              Chicago Joe's – 2256 W. Irving Park Rd.
TRIVIA   What world-famous band used to frequent the
              Fireplace Inn in the 1970s after concerts?

NOTES   _____

              _____

              _____

              _____

              _____

              _____

              _____

ANSWER: *The Rolling Stones.*

FIRESIDE RESTAURANT & LOUNGE

5739 N. Ravenswood Ave. (5800N, 1800W)
Chicago, IL 60660
(773) 561-7433

Website	www.firesidechicago.com
Neighborhood	Edgewater
Open 'til & Cover	4am (5am Sat); never a cover
Drinks	80 microbrews/imports, wines by glass
Food	Cajun-accented with ribs and pizza
Music	Internet jukebox
Bar Type	Neighborhood Tavern, Restaurant

Fireside is one of Chicago's oldest continuously operating taverns. The original owner, Peter Eberhardt, built the roadhouse in 1904 to serve farmers heading to the markets further south as well as mourners attending services across the street at the city's largest and one of the oldest graveyards, Rosehill Cemetery (1859). What is now a single building was originally constructed as twin buildings separated by a breezeway in between. The original wooden siding has been stuccoed over in the English Tudor style and the space between has been transformed into the pub's entrance. The tavern passed through many hands until Larry Staggs and Rich Wohn purchased it in 1989. Today, the off-the-beaten-path Fireside serves a Cajun-accented menu, highlighted by ribs and pizza. It's especially enjoyed in winter for its brick fireplace, in summer for its spacious beer garden, and by weekend brunch enthusiasts who appreciate the build-your-own Bloody Mary bar with over 120 hot sauces to choose from. Fireside is one of the few taverns in the area with a late-night license and the kitchen is open until just before closing. Fireside also attracts ghost hunters checking out the allegedly haunted Rosehill Cemetery that was actually named after tavernkeeper Hiram Roe. The land was originally known as Roe's Hill until a mapmaker misspelled it as "Rose Hill" and the rest is history.

NEARBY	Ravenswood Pub – 5455 N. Ravenswood Ave.
	Joie de Vine – 1744 W. Balmoral Ave.
	Joe's 2 and 6 Pub – 1818 W. Foster Ave.
SIMILAR	**OLDEST CITY TAVERNS**
	Schaller's Pump – 3714 S. Halsted St.
	17 West at the Berghoff – 17 W. Adams St.
	Green Mill Cocktail Lounge –
	4802 N. Broadway
	NEIGHBORHOOD SALOONS
	Southport City Saloon – 2548 N. Southport Ave.
	Twin Anchors – 1655 N. Sedgwick St.
	Green Door Tavern – 678 N. Orleans St.
TRIVIA	What Patrick Swayze movie featured Rosehill Cemetery in its climactic gunfight scene?

NOTES

_____

_____

_____

_____

_____

_____

ANSWER: Next of Kin *(1989).*

FOUR FARTHINGS TAVERN & GRILL

2060 N. Cleveland Ave. (2000N, 600W)
Chicago, IL 60614
(773) 935-2060

Website	www.fourfarthings.biz
Neighborhood	Lincoln Park
Open 'til & Cover	2am (3am Sat); never a cover
Drinks	12 beers on tap, up to 80 wines
Food	Steaks, pasta, seafood
Music	Classic rock jukebox
Bar Type	Neighborhood Tavern, Restaurant

The Four Farthings opened in 1968 and was originally frequented by beatniks and hippies alongside neighborhood
blue- and white-collar regulars. The pub takes its name from
the four provinces that make up The Shire in J.R.R. Tolkien's
fantasy classics, *The Hobbit* and *Lord of the Ring*s. These Shire
provinces were named after the four points of the compass:
Northfarthing, Southfarthing, Eastfarthing, and Westfarthing.
In Hobbitspeak, when you're at the Four Farthings, you are in
the center of the world where all farthings meet. Today, some
erroneously think that Four Farthings is a sports bar or an
Irish pub, like so many of the watering holes on Lincoln
Avenue. It actually offers an English pub atmosphere, complete with wooden paneling, old photographs, and antique fixtures. On the other hand, the Four Farthings does transform
into a lively singles scene for a somewhat older crowd (40+) as
the night wears on. The dining room was added in 1981,
when owners Jon and Bill Nordhem bought what previously
was Murray's Used Bookstore and turned it into a dining room
featuring upscale entrées served by a waitstaff decked out in
white dress shirts and ties. The popular weekend brunch is
served until 4pm and includes eight types of Eggs Benedict
and 16-ounce Bloody Marys. In the summer months, patrons
enjoy a pleasant afternoon or evening in the sidewalk café that
runs along both Cleveland Avenue and Dickens Drive.

NEARBY	River Shannon – 425 W. Armitage Ave.
	Sedgwick's – 1935 N. Sedgwick St.
	Gamekeepers – 1971 N. Lincoln Ave.
SIMILAR	**BEST BAR BRUNCH**
	Stanley's Kitchen & Tap – 1970 N. Lincoln Ave.
	Duffy's Tavern Grille – 420½ W. Diversey Pkwy.
	Four Moon Tavern – 1847 W. Roscoe St.
	OLDER LINCOLN PARK CROWD
	(SERVING FOOD)
	Black Duck – 1800 N. Halsted St.
	Southport City Saloon – 2548 N. Southport Ave.
	Jack's Bar & Grill – 2856 N. Southport Ave.
TRIVIA	Four farthings had what value in Olde England?
NOTES	_____
	_____
	_____
	_____
	_____
	_____
	_____

ANSWER: One penny.

FRIAR TUCK

3010 N. Broadway (3000N, 600W)
Chicago, IL 60657
(773) 327-5101

Website	www.friartuck3010.com
Neighborhood	Lakeview
Open 'til & Cover	2am (3am Sat); never a cover
Drinks	Cheap mini-pitcher deals on domestics
Food	None, use the house phone for delivery
Music	Eclectic jukebox, karaoke on Wed/Thu
Bar Type	Neighborhood Tavern, Dive Bar

Have you ever seen the bar on Broadway that looks like the top of a giant beer barrel sunken into the ground, next to where the Dominick's grocery store once burned down? This is your first introduction to the cheesy goodness of Friar Tuck. While somewhat foreboding on the outside with its narrow windows and heavy wood, Friar Tuck is instead a warm and inviting place on the inside. Pass through the giant cask and you'll find a long rectangular bar in the middle of the room where the regulars crowd when they're not in the coveted spots near the brick-enclosed fireplace or throwing darts on one of two regulation dartboards. A wall full of photos depicts many of the patrons you'll see there on any given night. The surprisingly friendly crowd and proprietors are what makes Friar Tuck endearing. Angelo and Christine Como opened the joint in 1970 and still run the place today, and many regulars have frequented the place for many years since then. Friar Tuck tradition: doing shots out of an inflatable sheep's hind quarters (if you know what I mean). Additional entertainment of a non-ovine nature is found on two video poker machines and karaoke every Wednesday and Thursday night. Friar Tuck's is also a great spot to observe the annual Gay Pride Parade in June, as the Comos set up a grill outside and sell Bahama Mamas and draft beers.

NEARBY	Monsignor Murphy's – 3019 N. Broadway
	Dram Shop – 3040 N. Broadway
	Wilde Bar & Restaurant – 3130 N. Broadway
SIMILAR	**FRIAR REFUGES**
	Monk's Pub – 205 W. Lake St.
	Hopleaf Bar – 5148 N. Clark St.
	Moody's Pub – 5910 N. Broadway
	DIVE BAR KARAOKE
	Louie's Pub – 1659 W. North Ave.
	Hidden Cove – 5336 N. Lincoln Ave.
	Carol's Pub – 4659 N. Clark St.
TRIVIA	According to Friar Tuck lore, what famous announcer fell down the stairs across the street at Fat Black Pussy Cat (now Monsignor Murphy's)?

NOTES _____

_____

_____

_____

_____

_____

ANSWER: *Bryant Gumble.*

GALE STREET INN

4914 N. Milwaukee Ave. (4900N, 5400W)
Chicago, IL 60630
(773) 725-1300

Website	www.galestreet.com
Neighborhood	Jefferson Park
Open 'til & Cover	10pm (10:30pm Fri/Sat, 9pm Sun); n/c
Drinks	Cold beer, martinis, retro cocktails
Food	Baby back ribs, steaks, chops, seafood
Music	The sound of rib bones hitting plates
Bar Type	Rib Joint, Neighborhood Tavern

Without the advantage of Miller's Pub's location or the celebrity caché of Twin Anchors, Gale Street Inn has endured as Jefferson Park's oldest and most popular tavern thanks to its fall-off-the-bone baby back ribs and for being "a regular place" in the neighborhood. Named for its nearest cross street, George Cholies opened Gale Street in January 1963, after being forced to abandon his sandwich shop and tavern across the street due to the construction of the Jefferson Park Transit Center for buses and the Blue Line "L" stop. Edward Fox Photography is located next door, another Chicago institution since 1902. Gale Street itself is named for Abram Gale, owner of the area's first wood frame house. Cholies sold Gale Street Inn in 1984 to the Karzas family, who still run it today. The story at Gale Street is the ribs, well known beyond the area from good exposure at the Taste of Chicago and North Center's Ribfest, but mostly from old-fashioned word-of-mouth. A full slab of ribs runs $22.95, with $4 off on Mondays. Patrons enjoy cocktails at the long wooden bar or dine beyond a frosted glass partition in a room with clinker brick and timber walls adorned with vintage Jefferson Park photos. The crowd consists primarily of neighborhood residents, cops from nearby Gale Street Station, and some O'Hare hotel traffic. As for Cholies, he opened another Gale Street Inn in Mundelein, with no connection to the original other than the name.

NEARBY   Jefferson Inn – 4874 N. Milwaukee Ave.
          Martini Club – 4935 N. Milwaukee Ave.
          Fischman's – 4776 N. Milwaukee Ave.

SIMILAR   **JEFFERSON PARK STAPLES**
          Ham Tree Inn – 5333 N. Milwaukee Ave.
          Vaughan's Pub – 5485 N. Northwest Hwy.
          Thatch Pub – 5707 N. Milwaukee Ave.
          CLASSIC RIB JOINTS
          Twin Anchors – 1655 N. Sedgwick St.
          Miller's Pub – 134 S. Wabash Ave.
          Chicago Joe's – 2256 W. Irving Park Rd.

TRIVIA   When was the town of Jefferson Park annexed
          to Chicago?

NOTES   _____

          _____

          _____

          _____

          _____

          _____

          _____

ANSWER: 1886, same year as Lake View & Hyde Park.

GINGERMAN TAVERN

3740 N. Clark St. (3800N, 1200W)
Chicago, IL 60613
(773) 549-2050

Website	None
Neighborhood	Wrigleyville
Open 'til & Cover	2am (3am Sat); never a cover
Drinks	15 beers on tap, 50 more in bottles
Food	None, unless you eat chalk
Music	Gnarliest jukebox east of the Kennedy
Bar Type	Neighborhood Tavern

The Gingerman Tavern has been a Wrigleyville landmark since 1977, a sort of antithesis of the sports bars that choke off the rest of the block (like its predecessor, Grand Slam Tavern). If the aquamarine neon sign in the window doesn't grab you, perhaps the purple sign depicting a woman lying with a breast exposed on the back of a black panther will... The Gingerman was named after J.P. Donleavy's first and often banned novel, *The Ginger Man* (1955), written about American ex-pat Sebastian Dangerfield and his amoral lifestyle in Dublin. As such, the Gingerman Tavern attracts a combination of Wrigleyville Bohemians (who knew?), beer lovers, pool sharks (two tables in the back), and the unlikely combination of post-game Cub fans mixed in with the heavily pierced and tattooed spillover from Metro next door. The Gingerman has a lone television set (sans ESPN) and they once played *Ride of the Valkyries* to ward off Cubbie Nation after games. Dan Schnitta owns the bar and also operates the GingerMan Raceway in South Haven, Michigan. If you're hungry, drop in across the street at Wrigleysville Dogs (yes, that is spelled correctly) for a gyro or a proper Chicago hot dog, as no food is served here. The Gingerman is a Wrigleyville staple and a classic Chicago neighborhood pub amidst the madness that surrounds Wrigley Field, something any sane hop or music enthusiast can appreciate.

NEARBY	Metro & Smart Bar – 3730 N. Clark St.
	Piano Man – 3801 N. Clark St.
	Uncommon Ground – 3800 N. Clark St.
SIMILAR	**NON-WEST SIDE BOHEMIA**
	Hungry Brain – 2319 W. Belmont Ave.
	Ten Cat – 3931 N. Ashland Ave.
	Leadway Bar & Grill – 5233 N. Damen Ave.
	POOL HALL PUBS
	Southport Lanes & Billiards –
	3325 N. Southport
	Seven Ten Lounge – 2747 N. Lincoln Ave.
	Dave & Buster's – 1030 N. Clark St.
TRIVIA	Gingerman has a cameo in what Scorsese film?
NOTES	_____
	_____
	_____
	_____
	_____
	_____
	_____

ANSWER: The Color of Money, with Paul Newman and Tom Cruise.

GLASCOTT'S GROGGERY

2158 N. Halsted St. (2200N, 800W)
Chicago IL, 60614
(773) 281-1205

Website	www.glascotts.com
Neighborhood	Lincoln Park
Open 'til & Cover	2am (3am Sat); never a cover
Drinks	15 beers on tap, a few wines
Food	Zip; Athenian Room next door (Greek)
Music	Decent jukebox played very loudly
Bar Type	Neighborhood Tavern, Sports Bar

Glascott's is located in a red-brick, three-flat in the heart of Lincoln Park. Once literally a meat market, the building later served as James Morley Soft Drinks during Prohibition. Can you say *speakeasy*? The groggery later opened in 1937 as Larry's Tavern, named after the original owner, Lawrence Glascott, who continued a family tradition that began when Irish immigrant Patrick Glascott opened a saloon in the late 1800s on Ashland Avenue. Lawrence Glascott once acquired a racing horse and kept it in the stables up the street and brought it over to his saloon to show it off. The regulars chided Glascott for leaving the equine outside so he brought in the beast and slapped it on the hindquarters to show how fast it could run... *inside* the bar. Because of unwelcome publicity following a shooting death right outside, the pub was later renamed Glascott's in 1971. Up until the 1980s, Glascott's catered to a rough set of neighborhood workers who'd come in for a shot and a beer before heading off to work—quite common in those days. Then came gentrification through Mayor Richard J. Daley's neighborhood revitalization projects of the '70s and the expansion of DePaul University. As it still is today, Glascott's soon became a party bar for young professionals and DePaul students, many of whom met, got married, and then fled to the suburbs. In keeping with tradition, the groggery remains family-owned by a constantly replenished supply of Glascotts who keep the dream alive.

NEARBY	Kelly's Pub – 949 W. Webster Ave.
	McGee's – 950 W. Webster Ave.
	Sterch's – 2238 N. Lincoln Ave.
SIMILAR	**LINCOLN PARK CLASSICS–COME–PARTY CENTRAL**
	Beaumont – 2020 N. Halsted St.
	John Barleycorn Mem. Pub – 658 W. Belden Ave.
	Burwood Tap – 724 W. Wrightwood Ave.
	LIVELY FORMER SPEAKEASIES
	Butch McGuire's – 20 W. Division St.
	Halligan Bar – 2274 N. Lincoln Ave.
	Durkin's – 810 W. Diversey Pkwy.
TRIVIA	What pro Chicago team has hosted parties here?

NOTES _____

_____

_____

_____

_____

_____

ANSWER: *Blackhawks (NHL).*

GOLD STAR BAR

1755 W. Division St. (1200N, 1800W)
Chicago, IL 60622
(773) 227-8700

Website	None
Neighborhood	Ukrainian Village
Open 'til & Cover	2am (3am Sat); never a cover
Drinks	Cheap beer, highlighted by Old Style
Food	Free popcorn and Tamale Guy visits
Music	An eclectic jukebox
Bar Type	Neighborhood Tavern, Dive, Haunted

In 1949, Chicago novelist and underground poet Nelson Algren painted the town red with the French philosopher Simone de Beauvoir (who was married to Jean Paul Sartre), and Gold Star was one of their prime boozing destinations. Division Street, then nicknamed "Polish Broadway," forms one leg of what was once called the Polish Triangle along with Ashland and Milwaukee avenues. In that colorful era, the Polish Triangle was filled with polka bars, gambling dens, and whorehouses, of which Gold Star offered two out of three (hint: no dice or cards). Not much is known about Gold Star from those days, but it is said that the old Polish lady who ran the place until 1990 actually took over when Prohibition ended in 1933. Prior to that, gangsters ran it as a speakeasy. As if inspired by Algren himself, Bohemian hipsters today flock to Gold Star Bar for cheap beer and pool, to relax on the finest lawn furniture and vinyl barstools that money won't buy, and to be entertained by a jukebox stocked with indie classics. Unframed works from local artists (sometimes Gold Star patrons) adorn the walls. Occasional ghost hunters also stop by for a glimpse of a girl in a lime green dress, a man in a straw hat, or the presence of the would-be hold-up guy shot by a bartender in the 1950s, according to Ursula Bielski in her book, *More Chicago Haunts: Scenes from Myth and Memory.* Perhaps this is why the gargoyle lurks above the bar?

NEARBY   Phyllis' Musical Inn – 1800 W. Division St.
Inner Town Pub – 1935 W. Thomas St.
Happy Village – 1059 N. Wolcott Ave.

SIMILAR   **CLASSIC BOHEMIAN DIVE BARS**
Rainbo Club – 1150 N. Damen Ave.
Old Town Ale House – 219 W. North Ave.
Weeds Tavern – 1555 N. Dayton St.
HAUNTED TAVERN LEGENDS
Bucktown Pub – 1658 W. Cortland St.
California Clipper – 1002 N. California Ave.
Guthries Tavern – 1300 W. Addison St.

TRIVIA   What Hollywood element can be found outside of Gold Star Bar?

NOTES   _____
_____
_____
_____
_____
_____
_____

ANSWER: A gold star in the sidewalk out front.

GOOSE ISLAND BREW PUB

1800 N. Clybourn Ave. (1800N, 1000W)
Chicago, IL 60614
(312) 915-0071

Website	www.gooseisland.com
Neighborhood	Lincoln Park
Open 'til & Cover	1am, 2am Fri/Sat, 11pm Sun; no cover
Drinks	16+ beers on tap: favorites & seasonal
Food	Locally sourced food that pairs with beers
Music	Occasional small live acts
Bar Type	Brew Pub, Neighborhood Tavern

Goose Island opened in 1988 to a public itching for something more than Budweiser, Miller Lite, and Heineken. The actual Goose Island lies just south on the Chicago River, believed to be named for the Irish squatters who raised livestock and, obviously, geese there. Chicago's first mayor, William B. Ogden, owned the land that previously occupied the river's east bank. By dredging a canal to extract clay, Ogden created the eastern side of the "new" island. The pub is instead located in a slice of Lincoln Park known as the R.A.N.C.H. Triangle as it is bordered by Racine, Armitage, North, the Chicago River, and Halsted. The area just south of the bar was known as Little Hell, due to area gashouse flames, a population of 30,000 ruffians, and 400 saloons. The Cabrini Green housing project was built in Little Hell in 1941 and became one of the most dangerous places in the country. Much of Cabrini has been torn down in the last decade, and the area around the pub is now filled with shops and restaurants. At the Goose, patrons quaff handcrafted brews at the mahogany, *Cheers*-like island bar. Favorites include Honker's Ale (brewed at their Fulton Street brewery), seasonal ales brewed onsite like oatmeal stout, Kölsch, and barley wine. About 50 are released each year. All of the above will help you earn an MBA (Master's of Beer Appreciation) offered by the bar. While their Wrigleyville location is hard to beat after a Cubs game, the original location remains a Chicago classic.

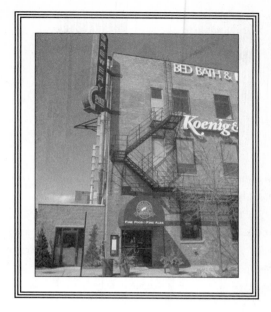

NEARBY	U.S. Beer Co. – 1801 N. Clybourn Ave.
	Kincade's – 950 W. Armitage Ave.
	Shoes Pub – 1134 W. Armitage Ave.
SIMILAR	**TOP BEER BARS BY TOTAL NUMBER OF BEERS**
	Hopleaf – 5148 N. Clark St. (308)
	Map Room – 1949 N. Hoyne Ave. (277)
	Quenchers Saloon – 2401 N. Western Ave. (261)
	CHICAGOLAND BREW PUBS
	Piece – 1927 W. North Ave.
	Revolution Brewing – 2323 N. Milwaukee Ave.
	Roundhouse – 205 N. Broadway (Aurora)
TRIVIA	What car protectant manufacturer once operated here?

NOTES

_____

_____

_____

_____

_____

_____

_____

ANSWER: *Turtle Wax.*

GREEN DOOR TAVERN

678 N. Orleans St. (700N, 300W)
Chicago, IL 60610
(312) 664-5496

Website	www.greendoorchicago.com
Neighborhood	River North
Open 'til & Cover	2am (3am Sat); never a cover
Drinks	The usual suspects (10 beers on tap)
Food	Good pub grub at hip restaurant prices
Music	A well-stocked jukebox
Bar Type	Neighborhood Tavern, Tourist Trap

Built in 1872 by James McCole, the Green Door Tavern is a true Chicago landmark. The building was one of the first constructed after the Great Chicago Fire of 1871, and the last wood frame building allowed this close to the Loop. After originally serving as a grocery store, the place became Vito Giacomoni's Huron-Orleans Restaurant in 1921. It passed to Vito's sons Jack and Nello, who operated the basement as a speakeasy during Prohibition—one of the first downtown— and attracted a clientele of Chicago gangsters. It's still in use today for theatrical performances. The nickname "Green Door" came into use during the 1930s and stuck, not only because of the front door's color, but also because "green door" was a euphemism for speakeasy back in the day. George Parenti bought 678 N. Orleans in 1985 and filled it with enough antique Americana to make the Smithsonian jealous, and which fascinates tourists, conventioneers, and suburbanites to this day. Over the years, the tavern has survived Prohibition, urban decay, a fire in 1989, a car crash, regular patronage of former Chicago Bull Dennis Rodman, and a wave of gentrification that claimed many older structures. Even the noticeable lean of the building is 100 years old. Television journalist Bill Kurtis is a regular, with his studio located behind the saloon, as are an increasing number of condo dwellers who descend upon the Green Door Tavern to watch the game at the Brunswick bar or to play pool in the side room.

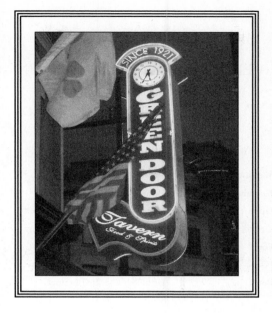

NEARBY	Club Lago – 331 W. Superior St.
	Hop Häus – 646 N. Franklin St.
	Brehon Pub – 731 N. Wells St.
SIMILAR	**TOURIST TRAPS**
	Billy Goat Tavern – 430 N. Michigan Ave.
	The Lodge – 21 W. Division St.
	Dick's Last Resort – 315 N. Dearborn St.
	TCHOTCHKE HEAVEN
	Burwood Tap – 724 W. Wrightwood Ave.
	Chicago Joe's – 2256 W. Irving Park Rd.
	Butch McGuire's – 20 W. Division St.
TRIVIA	What mythical beast can be found above the bar?
NOTES	

ANSWER: *The Jackalope.*

GREEN MILL COCKTAIL LOUNGE

4802 N. Broadway (4800N, 1200W)
Chicago, IL 60640
(773) 878-5552

Website	www.greenmilljazz.com
Neighborhood	Uptown
Open 'til & Cover	4am (5am Sat); $6–12 after 8pm
Drinks	Classic cocktails, domestic beer
Food	None (not even a bag of chips)
Music	Best jazz in the known universe
Bar Type	Jazz Club, Cocktail Lounge

After 100 years, the Green Mill still embodies the Jazz Age in which it was born. The club opened in 1907 as Pop Morse's Gardens (because of its sunken outdoor patio), and was a notable roadhouse stop for Chicagoans visiting St. Boniface's Cemetery. Tom Chamales bought it in 1910, erected a green windmill on the roof, and renamed it Green Mill Gardens. The inspiration came from the Moulin Rouge (Red Mill) in Paris, with *green* used to avoid confusion with the city's red light district (The Levee). Back then, Charlie Chaplin would stop by after filming at nearby Essanay Studios on Argyle Street, before Chicago's movie industry moved to Hollywood. The Green Mill was then leased to Al Capone's right-hand man, "Machine Gun" Jack McGurn, who orchestrated the St. Valentine's Day Massacre. Capone often came in, taking his favorite seat across from the bar so he could keep an eye on both doors. The Batsis Brothers acquired the Green Mill in 1942 and installed the present-day décor to attract upscale patrons, including Frank Sinatra after a meal at Twin Anchors (p. 186). Following a long descent into decrepitude culminating in its use as a heroin shooting gallery, the Green Mill's glory days were resurrected in 1986 by current owner Dave Jemilo, who restored the 40s décor, brought in the best jazz acts in the country, and hosted Marc Smith's Uptown Poetry Slam. Because of its rich history and classic ambience, the Green Mill has appeared in many films, including *The Untouchables*, *High Fidelity*, and the 80s television series, *Crime Story*.

NEARBY   Crew Bar + Grill – 4804 N. Broadway (gay)
              Fat Cat – 4840 N. Broadway
              Uptown Lounge – 1136 W. Lawrence Ave.

SIMILAR   **JAZZ CLUBS**
              Andy's Jazz Club – 11 E. Hubbard St.
              BackRoom – 1007 N. Rush St.
              Green Dolphin Street – 2200 N. Ashland Ave.
              NOTABLE COCKTAIL LOUNGES
              Coq d'Or – 140 E. Walton St. (Drake Hotel)
              Signature Lounge – 875 N. Michigan Ave.,
                96th Fl.
              Pump Room – 1301 N. State Pkwy.

TRIVIA   When did the Moulin Rouge open in Paris?

NOTES   _____

              _____

              _____

              _____

              _____

              _____

              _____

GUTHRIES TAVERN

1300 W. Addison St. (3600N, 1300W)
Chicago, IL 60613
(773) 477-2900

Website	None
Neighborhood	Wrigleyville
Open 'til & Cover	2am (3am Sat); never a cover
Drinks	Intriguing imports and microbrews
Food	Microwave, delivery encouraged
Music	CDs played by bartenders
Bar Type	Neighborhood Tavern, Haunted

For over 20 years, Guthries has been an inviting neighborhood tavern with character, in contrast to the cookie-cutter sterility plaguing so many newer establishments. Since Prohibition ended in 1933, the joint founded by the Moretti Family has operated as various watering holes, including a gay Latin biker bar prior to its opening as Guthries Tavern in 1986. The bar was either named after J.B. Guthrie, a prominent late-1800s developer in the Lakeview neighborhood (of which Wrigleyville is a part), or the owner's dog at the time—or both. Though Guthries is located three blocks west of Wrigley Field, you'll encounter no Cubs paraphernalia here and only a few small TVs. Instead, you'll find a bevy of board games, an impressive beer selection, and eclectic décor highlighted by a drop ceiling with panels decorated by local artists (à la Mutiny, p 134), Roman wainscoting, and paintings of nautical and wildlife scenes. If you're hungry, the bartender may be coaxed into microwaving you a pizza or White Castle Slider, but drawing a delivery menu from the metal bucket bursting with them is the wiser alternative. Better yet: Wait for the nightly appearance of the Tamale Guy. As a special treat for the waitstaff, Guthries is haunted by the spirit of a former owner who died on the premises. The apparition only makes its presence known after hours, similar to those apparitions found at Hangge Uppe (p. 84), Ole St. Andrew's, and Bucktown Pub, leaving patrons to focus their worries on the Cubs.

NEARBY   All bars around Wrigley Field and those along
the Southport Corridor (dozens)

SIMILAR   **PROHIBITION-ERA NEIGHBORHOOD TAVERNS**
Burwood Tap – 724 W. Wrightwood Ave.
Jake's Pub – 2932 N. Clark St.
Kelly's Pub – 949 W. Webster Ave.
BOARD GAMES
Newport Bar & Grill – 1344 W. Newport Ave.
Blue Frog – 676 N. LaSalle St.
Beachwood Inn – 1415 N. Wood St.

TRIVIA   Where and when was White Castle created?

NOTES   _____

_____

_____

_____

_____

_____

_____

_____

ANSWER: Wichita, Kansas, in 1921, making White Castle the
country's oldest hamburger chain.

HALF SHELL

676 W. Diversey Pkwy. (2800N, 700W)
Chicago, IL 60614
(773) 549-1773

Website	www.halfshellchicago.com
Neighborhood	Lakeview
Open 'til & Cover	10:30pm (possibly earlier); no cover
Drinks	Cheap beer pitchers, basic well
Food	Seafood, king crab leg specialty
Music	Wall-mounted jukebox, rarely played
Bar Type	Dive Bar, Oyster Bar

Around the time my parents' generation was getting a Chicago police beat-down during the Democratic National Convention, Dan Denizman opened the Half Shell pub and oyster bar—not a bad choice a former commodore of the Chicago Yachting Association. His daughter Candice now runs Half Shell, but not much has changed since 1969 except the prices (and not by that much). King crab legs are still the specialty and are often featured with snow crab legs for $26. Many also love the Dungeness crab, Blue Point oysters, Cherrystone clams, and soft shell crab tempura (when in season). Patrons wash down their shellfish bounty with $12 domestic pitchers. Though Half Shell's underground lair is just large enough to accommodate a bar and a dozen tables, the kitchen serves up more than three tons of seafood per week. An additional bonus is the sidewalk café, where the people watching along Diversey in summer rivals that of Mickey's (Lincoln Park), Dublin's (Gold Coast), and Moonshine (Wicker Park). Signs, signs, everywhere a sign: *Only cash is accepted, Men are prohibited from wearing a hat inside* (thanks to a Turkish dinner custom), and *Indoor seating arrangements are made exclusively by the bartender* (an occasionally crotchety chap named Alex who has worked at Half Shell for almost 30 years). While it is mostly popular with locals in the know, Half Shell also attracts the occasional celebrity, including Al Pacino, Sandra Bullock, Julia Roberts, and Cubs players.

NEARBY	Matisse – 674 W. Diversey Pkwy. (next door)
	Firkin & Pheasant – 670 W. Diversey Pkwy.
	Durkin's – 810 W. Diversey Pkwy.
SIMILAR	**SEAFOOD TAVERNS**
	Raw Bar & Grill – 3720 N. Clark St.
	King Crab – 1816 N. Halsted St.
	Cy's Crab House – 3819 N. Ashland Ave.
	SUBTERRANEAN CLASSICS
	Redhead Piano Bar – 16 W. Ontario St.
	Underground Wonder Bar – 10 E. Walton St.
	Mother's, The Original – 26 W. Division St.
TRIVIA	What creature does Half Shell's logo belong to?
NOTES	_____
	_____
	_____
	_____
	_____
	_____
	_____
	_____
	_____

ANSWER: *The sea scallop.*

HAMILTON'S BAR & GRILL

6341 N. Broadway (6400N, 1200W)
Chicago, IL 60660
(773) 764-8133

Website	www.hamiltonsbarandgrill.com
Neighborhood	Edgewater
Open 'til & Cover	2am (3am Sat); cover $2–3
Drinks	Cheap beer (stick with bottles)
Food	Greasy burgers and pizza
Music	Good jukebox, weekend DJs
Bar Type	Neighborhood Tavern, College Bar

Though it has been around since 1933, Hamilton's Pub was unlikely to be mentioned in any historical Chicago texts until now... Not much is known about Hamilton's from its early days, other than that Richard Doan & Sons ran it for many years and that its original Depression-era décor was remodeled in the mid-'80s. Jerry Sheehy now runs the joint and has further remodeled the place, making Hamilton's a little more pub-like (at least on the outside). Given its proximity to Loyola University, "Hammy's" is everything you'd want in a college bar: it's spacious, offers cheap booze and greasy pub grub, and has a long history of helping local students forget about their studies. While more seasoned barflies might bypass the boisterous nightly crowd that makes those in their mid-20s feel old, Hamilton's attracts Loyola students in droves, particularly with daily specials that go easy on the collegiate budget, as well as the wallets of locals and tradesmen at lunchtime. The ancient Hamilton's Lounge sign, wet T-shirt contests, and flame-blowing bartenders have all gone the way of Nelson Brothers (*loves me, and they love you too...*), but Hamilton's is still an entertaining place to get your drink on and watch Rambler basketball. Throw in a certain kind of charm that only a 75-year-old pub can possess and you've got a bonafide Chicago classic that is here to stay.

NEARBY   Sovereign – 6202 N. Broadway

Pumping Company – 6157 N. Broadway

Moody's Pub – 5910 N. Broadway

SIMILAR   SATURDAY NIGHT, BEER-SOAKED DANCE PARTY

She-nannigan's House of Beer –
16 W. Division St.

Hangge Uppe – 4 W. Elm St.

The Apartment – 2251 N. Lincoln Ave.

CLASSIC COLLEGE PUBS

Kelly's Pub – 949 W. Webster Ave. (DePaul)

Hawkeye's – 1458 W. Taylor St. (UIC)

Woodlawn Tap – 1172 E. 55th St.
(University of Chicago)

TRIVIA   Loyola University became the only Illinois college to win the men's NCAA tournament in what year?

NOTES   _____

_____

_____

_____

_____

ANSWER: 1963.

HANGGE UPPE

14 W. Elm St. (1150N, 0W)
Chicago, IL 60610
(312) 337-0561

Website	www.rushanddivision.com
Neighborhood	Gold Coast
Open 'til & Cover	4am (5am Sat); $10 cover
Drinks	Beer tubs and kamikaze shots
Food	Free popcorn
Music	Retro downstairs, urban dance upstairs
Bar Type	Nightclub, Meat Market, Late-Night

When I ask people if they've been to Hangge Uppe, I always get the same reaction: a downcast look, slight nod of the head, and sheepish "yes." It's what I call the "Hangge Uppe Face." To many, particularly visitors to Chicago and bachelorette party-goers, Hangge Uppe is a late-night blast. Stay too late though, and it could become your own personal *Nightmare on Elm Street*. Either way, arrive before midnight and you'll avoid a half-hour wait to get in. Step inside and you'll find modern beats on the dance floor upstairs and a retro sing-a-long throughout the catacombs downstairs—every night of the week. The first of four bars in the basement is the Watermelon Bar, which is reputedly haunted by a young woman killed when the place served as a speakeasy during Prohibition. The apparition likes to drop ashtrays, open taps, and overturn chairs after hours. Venturing further into the bowels of Hangge Uppe, the Island Bar lies across from the bathrooms and was were you would find a man named Leon dispensing "useless advice" every Fri/Sat night since the place opened in 1973. Sadly, Leon has gone to the Big Hangge Uppe in the Sky, so ask for a "Sleeper" cocktail in his honor on your next visit. Other celebrity guests have included Vince Vaughn and Mickey Mantle; Chris Farley was reputed to have spent his last night here. All in all, Hangge Uppe is the most colorful of the Lodge Management Group holdings that began with The Lodge (p. 112).

NEARBY   Elm Street Liquors – 14 W. Elm St.
Zebra Lounge – 1120 N. State Pkwy.
The Lodge – 21 W. Division St.

SIMILAR   **CHEESEBALL DANCE PARTY**
She-nannigan's House of Beer – 16 W. Division
Mother's, The Original – 26 W. Division St.
Excalibur Nightclub – 632 N. Dearborn St.
LESSER KNOWN TAVERN HAUNTINGS
Fireplace Inn – 1448 N. Wells St.
Guthries Tavern – 1300 W. Addison St.
Edgewater Lounge – 5600 N. Ashland Ave.

TRIVIA   How do you make a Sleeper?

NOTES   _____

_____

_____

_____

_____

_____

_____

HEARTLAND CAFÉ

7000 N. Glenwood Ave. (7000N, 1400W)
Chicago, IL 60626
(773) 465-8005

Website	www.heartlandcafe.com
Neighborhood	Rogers Park
Open 'til & Cover	2am (3am Sat); $6 cover for bands
Drinks	A baker's dozen on tap, more in bottles
Food	Buffalo burgers, vegetarian, brunch
Music	Live jazz, folk, reggae (Wed–Sun)
Bar Type	Neighborhood Tavern, Restaurant

Michael James and Katie Hogan opened this Rogers Park institution in August 1976, in what was once a steakhouse—ironic, as they are now anti-beef. Today, the Heartland Café is a critically-acclaimed community restaurant and bar where the socially-conscious are welcome, along with the rest of us who have sold out and revel in the material world. Though you may need to practice your patience waiting for your order, the intriguing selection of hippie chow, ranging from their hugely popular brunch to buffalo burgers to a number of vegetarian dishes, is worth the wait. Add to that the surprisingly good selection of microbrews served in their Buffalo Bar, a killer sidewalk café, and a general store (where you can get your kicks in the photo booth, find a Che Guevara T-shirt, or pick up some Remember the Haymarket Riots temporary tattoos), and you've got a classic piece of the Chicago puzzle. The Heartland has hosted countless political forums, including early speeches by Illinois congressmen Paul Simon, Jesse Jackson Jr., and Barack Obama. Loyola University's WLUW 88.7 FM broadcasts *Live from the Heartland* every Saturday morning from 9am to 10am, covering local social issues. The adjacent Red Line Tap is under the same ownership and was renovated following Roy Kawaguchi's passing in 1996. "Roy's" dates back to the early 1900s and served as taverns named the 7006 Club and Rogers Park Boating.

NEARBY	Red Line Tap – 7006 N. Glenwood Ave.
	The Glenwood – 6962 N. Glenwood Ave.
	Duke's Hideaway – 6920 N. Glenwood Ave.
SIMILAR	**FULL-SERVICE NEIGHBORHOOD JOINTS**
	Club Lucky – 1824 W. Wabansia Ave.
	John Barleycorn Memorial Pub –
	658 W. Belden Ave.
	Chicago Brauhaus – 4732 N. Lincoln Ave.
	ONE-TIME HIPPIE HAVENS
	Old Town Ale House – 219 W. North Ave.
	Sterch's – 2238 N. Lincoln Ave.
	Four Farthings – 2060 N. Cleveland Ave.
TRIVIA	Who led the "Chicago Seven," the group charged for inciting the 1968 DNC riots?
NOTES	_____
	_____
	_____
	_____
	_____
	_____

ANSWER: *Abbie Hoffman.*

HIDEOUT

1354 W. Wabansia Ave. (1700N, 1400W)
Chicago, IL 60622
(773) 227-4433

Website	www.hideoutchicago.com
Neighborhood	Back of Beyond (closest to Bucktown)
Open 'til & Cover	2am (3am Sat); $10 or less
Drinks	Whiskey, bottled and canned beer
Food	Beer nuts & pretzels, if you're lucky
Music	Regional indie rock and bluegrass
Bar Type	Neighborhood Tavern, Music Venue

What once looked like the house in *Texas Chainsaw Massacre*, actually couldn't be more inviting, thanks to the great people and music inside (and a recent renovation). Named because of its obscure location next to the Chicago Department of Fleet Management—that's where the city's 1,000 snow plows lie in wait for the next blizzard—the Hideout is the urban equivalent of Al Capone's Hideaway, the latter of which is located deep in the woods near suburban St. Charles on the Fox River. The building was originally constructed in the nineteenth century by "ditch-digging Irishmen with dirty boots and hats, always hats, pushed aside by the nickel and dime Prohibition-era Sicilian button men," according to Hideout management. Reputedly a speakeasy in those days, "where the '26 girls rolled the dice for dances and 10 cent drinks," the Hideout later appealed to the shot-and-a-beer-before-work crowd—ah, the good old days… In 1996, the husband and wife team of Tim Tuten and Katie Nicholson, together with twins Mike and Jim Hinchsliff, took over the Hideout and turned it into a hip live music venue to rival those mentioned below. Be sure to catch house band *Sanctified Grumblers* on Tuesday nights. The Hideout is not so hidden anymore to Chicagoans in the know, and routine mentions in the likes of *Rolling Stone* and *New York Times*, and their annual outreach program at *South by Southwest* in Austin, Texas, extend their aura.

NEARBY   Exit – 1315 W. North Ave.
Louie's Pub – 1659 W. North Ave.
Bucktown Pub – 1658 W. Cortland St.

SIMILAR   **PROHIBITION-ERA NEIGHBORHOOD TAVERNS**
Burwood Tap – 724 W. Wrightwood Ave.
Jake's Pub – 2932 N. Clark St.
Kelly's Pub – 949 W. Webster Ave.
LEGENDARY LOCAL LIVE MUSIC VENUES
Schubas Tavern – 3159 N. Southport Ave.
Elbo Room – 2871 N. Lincoln Ave.
Mutiny – 2428 N Western Ave. (punk)

TRIVIA   "When I Been Drinkin'," covered by Devil in a
Woodpile, was originally by which musician?

NOTES   _____

_____

_____

_____

_____

_____

_____

ANSWER: *Early 1900s bluesman Big Bill Broonzy.*

JAKE'S PUB

2932 N. Clark St. (3000N, 700W)
Chicago, IL 60657
(773) 248-3318

Website	www.jakespub.net
Neighborhood	Lakeview
Open 'til & Cover	2am (3am Sat); never a cover
Drinks	Surprising bottled beer selection (50)
Food	Nada
Music	Average jukebox
Bar Type	Neighborhood Tavern, Haunted, Dive

What would become Jake's Pub initially came into the world as a candy store operated by Jake Rosenbloom, a convenient front during Prohibition for the speakeasy next door. Look past the bar and you can still see the original candy store shelving in the back room. Once the Volstead Act was repealed on December 5, 1933, Rosenbloom renamed the place after himself and obtained one of the city's first liquor licenses. Jake's sons later took over the business and even started a bartending school after World War II to teach returning GIs a new trade. In the early 1970s, Jake's Pub was sold to one of the bar's regulars, Bob Toothman, who ran the place for 15 years and literally called the place home, sleeping on a cot in the backroom just as the original Jake had done. Following the precedent set before him, Toothman passed the baton to bar regular Scott Johnson, who has since transformed the pub from an old-man's bar into a modern neighborhood tavern, appealing to the multi-generational crowd now living in the area—several of whom have been immortalized in the drawings and photos hanging on the wall. Jake's Pub is also one of the few remaining dog-friendly establishments, as our city elders increasingly frown upon this practice. Drop by on Saturday night enough times and Hank Arnold, Jake's oldest regular, just might take a Polaroid of you for the Wall of Fame.

NEARBY	Duke of Perth – 2913 N. Clark St.
	Avenue Tavern – 2916 N. Broadway
	Matisse – 674 W. Diversey Pkwy.
SIMILAR	**NORTH SIDE PROHIBITION-ERA TAVERNS**
	Burwood Tap – 724 W. Wrightwood Ave.
	Kelly's Pub – 949 W. Webster Ave.
	Guthries Tavern – 1300 W. Addison St.
	DOG-FRIENDLY PUBS
	Charleston – 2076 N. Hoyne Ave.
	Lemmings – 1850 N. Damen Ave.
	Ten Cat Tavern – 3931 N. Ashland Ave.
TRIVIA	What Old Town institution also features artwork memorializing the regulars?
NOTES	_____
	_____
	_____
	_____
	_____
	_____
	_____

ANSWER: Old Town Ale House.

JAZZ SHOWCASE

806 S. Plymouth Ct. (800S, 50W)
Chicago, IL 60605
(312) 360-0234

Website	www.jazzshowcase.com
Neighborhood	Printers Row
Open 'til & Cover	1am (every day); $20–25 (cash only)
Drinks	Classic cocktails, domestic beer
Food	Just the olives in your martini
Music	Traditional jazz
Bar Type	Jazz Club, Cocktail Lounge

Chicago's most nomadic jazz club is also one of its finest. Since 1947, Joe Segal has been the Godfather of Chicago Jazz with his ever-persistent club, Jazz Showcase, which has hosted such jazz legends as Duke Ellington, John Coltrane, and Dizzy Gillespie. From its origins in the Gold Coast to ping-ponging from Lincoln Park to the South Loop (in the Blackstone Hotel) to River North, Jazz Showcase has found a new South Loop home in Printers Row, in historic Dearborn Station. For you train buffs, the Romanesque Revival building housing Dearborn Station and its unique 12-story tower were completed in 1885. The Santa Fe Railway ran trains from here to Hollywood from 1920 until 1971 and, as cars and airplanes eroded rail transportation, all remaining lines were consolidated at nearby Union Station. Like the printing business around it, the next 15 years ushered in an era of urban decay until Dearborn Station was converted into commercial office space as part of the revitalization of Printers Row. Today, Dearborn Station is one of the oldest train stations in the United States (albeit without a functioning train), making it a fitting home for one of Chicago's oldest jazz clubs. With 3,500 square feet, the latest Jazz Showcase is quite roomy and offers great sightlines to some of the best traditional jazz acts from the city and around the world. Consider a visit during Chicago's annual Jazz Festival held every Labor Day weekend (if not sooner).

NEARBY   Bar Louie Printers Row – 47 W. Polk St.
Kasey's Tavern – 701 S. Dearborn St.
Blackie's – 755 S. Clark St.

SIMILAR   **JAZZ CLUBS**
Andy's Jazz Club – 11 E. Hubbard St.
BackRoom – 1007 N. Rush St.
Green Mill Jazz Club – 4802 N. Broadway
HISTORIC LOCATIONS
Motel Bar – Montgomery Ward Building
Signature Lounge – Hancock Building
The Pub – Univ. of Chicago (students only)

TRIVIA   What famous jazz musician refused to play at
Jazz Showcase when it was in the Blackstone
Hotel?

NOTES   _____

_____

_____

_____

_____

_____

JOHN BARLEYCORN MEMORIAL PUB

658 W. Belden Ave. (2300N, 700W)
Chicago, IL 60614
(773) 348-8899

Website	www.johnbarleycorn.com
Neighborhood	Lincoln Park
Open 'til & Cover	2am (3am Sat); never a cover
Drinks	32 beers on tap, bevy of booze & wine
Food	Burgers, sandwiches, salads
Music	Good jukebox that gets louder, later
Bar Type	Neighborhood Tavern, Sports Bar

No other bar in Chicago can match the storied past, special décor, and general vibe of John Barleycorn Memorial Pub. The building dates back to 1890 when an Irish immigrant (surprise) opened the original saloon. During Prohibition, a Chinese laundry operated in front and a speakeasy in back, with liquor brought in under dirty clothes in laundry carts. During the Depression, John Dillinger frequented the joint and bought rounds for the house with his nefarious gains, before being gunned down in an alley next to the Biograph Theater, a few blocks north. The tavern was purchased in 1965 by Eric J. Van Gelder, a Dutchman with a penchant for handmade model ships, mahogany wood paneling, and projecting slides of 5,000 Art Institute pieces for the edification of his guests. Gelder opened his pub in the spirit of nineteenth–century England where, "drunkenness was so common as to go virtually unnoticed." He named it John Barleycorn after the personification of barley (as used in beer), a term first used in a ballad by Scotland's favorite son, Robert Burns. Barleycorn's, as locals know it today, is owned by Sam Sanchez, who continues the tradition with tasty half-pound burgers and a spacious beer garden. Additional locations have opened in Wrigleyville and suburban Schaumburg, and rumor has it that a new Barleycorn Bridgeport may open, replacing Jimbo's Lounge as the closest bar to U.S. Cellular Field, home to the Chicago White Sox.

NEARBY   Halligan Bar – 2274 N. Lincoln Ave.
Kelsey's – 2265 N. Lincoln Ave.
Kendall's – 2263 N. Lincoln Ave.

SIMILAR   **ANGLOPHILE NORTH SIDE CLASSICS**
Globe Pub – 1934 W. Irving Park Rd.
Four Farthings – 2060 N. Cleveland Ave.
Lion Head Pub – 2251 N. Lincoln Ave.
TOP LINCOLN PARK BEER GARDENS
Mickey's – 2450 N. Clark St.
Goodbar – 2512 N. Halsted St.
Charlie's on Webster – 1224 W. Webster Ave.

TRIVIA   John Barleycorn was captured on film in what
1996 Richard Gere movie?

NOTES   _____
_____
_____
_____
_____
_____
_____
_____

ANSWER: Primal Fear.

KASEY'S TAVERN

701 S. Dearborn St. (700N, 100W)
Chicago, IL 60605
(312) 427-7992

Website	www.kaseystavern.com
Neighborhood	Printers Row
Open 'til & Cover	2am (3am Sat); never a cover
Drinks	19 beers on tap, up to 150 in bottles
Food	Burgers from neighbor Hackney's
Music	Good jukebox
Bar Type	Neighborhood Tavern

Kasey's opened in 1974 but the building has reputedly housed pubs since 1889 when the original publisher of Frank L. Baum's *The Wizard of Oz*, M.A. Donohue & Co., constructed the building. Back then, the neighborhood was known as the Custom House Levee District and featured 37 bordellos and 46 saloons—including the Lone Star Saloon and Palm Garden, both run by Mickey Finn. An ex-pickpocket, Finn would drop sodium chloride into the drink of his victims who would then pass out (up to 2–3 days), be dragged into the back room, have their pockets rifled through, and be disposed of on the street. To slip someone a "Mickey" has since become synonymous for any knockout potion. Fast-forward to the Ford administration when Printers Row was full of publishers and print houses, and the original Kasey ran his tavern from dawn until dusk to accommodate typesetters working the night shift. Kasey sold the place in 1989 to local real estate maven, Bill White. Once offering penny pitchers for students from nearby Roosevelt University, Columbia College, and DePaul's South Loop campus, Kasey's now offers a huge microbrew selection and a sidewalk café to new neighborhood residents. Kasey's is also a sought after spot during the Printers Row Book Fair held annually in June and after 16" softball games in Grant Park. As the drinks go down, remember: "Be nice or be gone"—the strictly enforced motto of Kasey's Tavern.

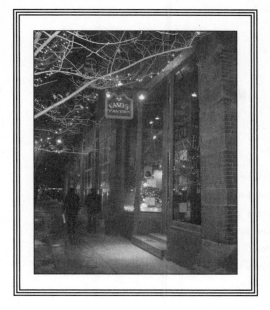

NEARBY   Hackney's – 733 S. Dearborn Pkwy.
Bar Louie – 3557 N. Clark St.
Blackie's – 755 S. Clark St.

SIMILAR   **HISTORIC NEIGHBORHOOD DIVES**
Old Town Ale House – 219 W. North Ave.
Bob Inn – 2609 W. Fullerton Ave.
Cork Lounge – 1822 W. Addison St.
FAUX IRISH SPORTS BARS
Schaller's Pump – 3714 S. Halsted St.
Chicago Blarney Stone – 3424 N. Sheffield Ave.
She-nannigan's House of Beer –
16 W. Division St.

TRIVIA   What other Chicago bar proclaims, "Positively
No Dancing," the second of Kasey's two mottos?

NOTES   _____

_____

_____

_____

_____

_____

ANSWER: Twin Anchors in Lincoln Park.

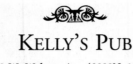

KELLY'S PUB

949 W. Webster Ave. (2000N, 1000W)
Chicago, IL 60614
(773) 281-0656

Website	www.kellyspub.com
Neighborhood	Lincoln Park
Open 'til & Cover	2am (3am Sat); never a cover
Drinks	Cheap beer
Food	Pub grub pumped out of a tiny kitchen
Music	Average jukebox
Bar Type	Neighborhood Tavern, College Bar

Kelly's Pub is the oldest continuously run tavern on the North Side. The space operated as a confectionary during Prohibition and wooden cabinetry from that era is still used behind the bar. When Prohibition ended, the joint was christened L-Side Tavern for its location adjacent to the "L," but it's been Kelly's Pub since its 1935 re-naming. Throughout the '70s, this part of Lincoln Park was crime-ridden until DePaul University expanded and Mayor Richard J. Daley began his Park West gentrification efforts. Photos of these dark days are found on the walls, near photos of the ecstasy—and ultimate agony—of DePaul's NCAA Men's Basketball Championship run in 1979, led by beloved coach Ray Meyer, a Kelly's regular. A small beer garden, curiously located under the "L," was built for a scene in *About Last Night* (1986) with Rob Lowe and Demi Moore. Kelly's Pub has also served as the official campus of fictitious Maguire University since 1988. Maguire U dates back to 1963 when Chicago's Loyola University won the NCAA Championship, and was "founded" by friends of Kelly's Pub owner, John Kelly, and patrons of Maguire's Pub in Forest Park (now closed). Maguire U was formalized in the early '70s to scam Final Four tickets from the NCAA, successfully achieved for two years until Bill Jauss exposed the scheme in the *Chicago Tribune*. Today, Maguire U obtains tickets via legitimate means (www.maguireuniversity.com).

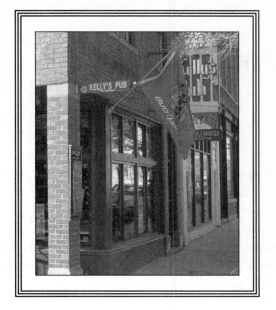

NEARBY	McGee's – 950 W. Webster Ave.
	Glascott's Groggery – 2158 N. Halsted Ave.
	Local Option – 1102 W. Webster Ave.
SIMILAR	**PROHIBITION-ERA NEIGHBORHOOD TAVERNS**
	Guthries Tavern – 1300 W. Addison St.
	Burwood Tap – 724 W. Wrightwood Ave.
	Jake's Pub – 2932 N. Clark St.
	CLASSIC COLLEGE PUBS
	Hamilton's – 6341 N. Broadway (Loyola)
	Hawkeye's – 1458 W. Taylor St. (UIC)
	Woodlawn Tap – 1172 E. 55th St.
	(University of Chicago)
TRIVIA	John Kelly's wife, Polly, started what summer
	neighborhood institution in 1969?
NOTES	_____
	_____
	_____
	_____
	_____
	_____

ANSWER: The Sheffield Garden Walk.

KINGSTON MINES

2548 N. Halsted St. (2600N, 800W)
Chicago, IL 60614
(773) 477-4646

Website	www.kingstonmines.com
Neighborhood	Lincoln Park
Open 'til & Cover	4am (5am Sat); $12–20 cover
Drinks	Bottled domestic beer and cocktails
Food	Kitchen window called Doc's Rib Joint
Music	Chicago Blues, a mix of urban & Delta
Bar Type	Blues Club

Kingston Mines opened in a former machine shop on Lincoln Avenue in 1968 by Lenin "Doc" Pellegrino, a physician by day. The initial format was a coffeehouse that featured more plays than blues acts, including the first production of the musical *Grease* in 1971. Bands initially played the Delta Blues (sorrowful country blues), but their sound evolved into a unique urban blues style…and the "Chicago Blues Center" was born. In 1980, the club's roof caved in (literally) and The Mines moved to River North, where the Blues Brothers, John Belushi and Dan Aykroyd, performed to promote their upcoming film. When the landlord doubled the rent, Kingston Mines moved to its current location on Halsted Street in 1982, replacing a jazz club named Redford's and forming the second half of "Blues Alley" with B.L.U.E.S. (p. 16) across the street. Today, Kingston Mines attracts locals, suburbanites, tourists from around the world, and celebrities alike, all of whom come for blues played continuously from 9:30pm to 3:30am, every night, alternating between two stages. Kingston Mines almost exclusively features local bands, like Magic Slim, A.C. Reed, and John Primer, but also occasionally draws such world-famous musicians as Mick Jagger and Bob Dylan. Even Eric Clapton is rumored to visit when he's in town, wearing a disguise. Be sure to get here early (or late) to get a seat.

NEARBY	B.L.U.E.S. – 2548 N. Halsted St.
	Burwood Tap – 724 W. Wrightwood Ave.
	Victory Liquors – 2610 N. Halsted St.

SIMILAR   **BLUES CLUBS, FARTHER AFIELD**

Rosa's Lounge – 3420 W. Armitage Ave.

Buddy Guy's Legends – 754 S. Wabash Ave.

New Checkerboard Lounge – 5201 S. Harper Ct.

CLASSIC CHICAGO MUSIC VENUES

Jazz Showcase – 806 S. Plymouth Ct. (jazz)

Empty Bottle – 1035 N. Western Ave.
(alternative)

Chicago Brauhaus – 4732 N. Lincoln Ave.
(German)

TRIVIA   What was the original title of *Grease*, based on the playwright's experience at Chicago's William H. Taft High School?

NOTES   _____

                   _____

                   _____

                   _____

                   _____

ANSWER: Grease Lightning.

KITTY O'SHEA'S

720 S. Michigan Ave. (lobby of Hilton Chicago)
Chicago, IL 60605
(312) 922-4400

Website	www.hilton.com
Neighborhood	South Loop
Open 'til & Cover	1am (2am Fri/Sat); never a cover
Drinks	A mean pint of Guinness for a hotel
Food	Fish & chips, Shepherd's Pie
Music	Live Irish (or rock) nightly
Bar Type	Hotel Bar, Irish Pub

Cead Mile Failte or "100,000 welcomes" is the mantra of Kitty O'Shea's, a fine Irish pub and lobby bar reminiscent of Knightsbridge Bar at the Arlington Hotel in Dublin. The décor, Irish nosh, properly pulled pint o' the Black Stuff, and waitstaff imported from Eire all make for a brilliant setting. The crowd consists of businessfolk and tourists staying at the hotel, except for election nights when top city Democrats are often spotted. Kitty O'Shea's is also popular after Bears games, due to its proximity to Soldier Field. The Chicago Hilton & Towers was the largest hotel in the world when it was built in 1927. A few highlights of the hotel's history are its serving as a World War II army barracks, being the epicenter of the 1968 DNC riots, and having a role in the film, *The Fugitive* (1993). Who was Kitty O'Shea? The downfall of Charles Stewart Parnell. Known as the "Uncrowned King of Ireland," Parnell agitated for Irish independence as a member of British Parliament from 1875–91, predating the Easter Uprising of 1918. After a failed blackmail attempt by her husband, it was revealed that Parnell lived with Katherine O'Shea while still married to William O'Shea. The perceived adultery greatly diminished Parnell's leadership. As he tried to regain control, he contracted pneumonia while giving an outdoor speech. He passed away in 1891 at the age of 45, in the arms of his wife Kitty who he had married three months earlier.

NEARBY   Lakeside Green Lounge – 720 S. Michigan Ave.
                   (lobby)
              Buddy Guy's Legends – 754 S. Wabash Ave.
              South Loop Club – 701 S. State St.

SIMILAR   **DOWNTOWN IRISH**
              Poag Mahone's – 333 S. Wells St.
              The Gage – 24 S. Michigan Ave.
              Kasey's Tavern – 701 S. Dearborn St.
              NOTABLE HOTEL BARS
              Pump Room – 1301 N. State (Ambassador East)
              Coq d'Or – 140 E. Walton St. (Drake Hotel)
              Lockwood – 17 E. Monroe St. (Palmer House)

TRIVIA   Helicopter landings on the roof of the Hilton
              & Towers were filmed for what TV series?

NOTES   _____

              _____

              _____

              _____

              _____

              _____

ANSWER: ER.

L&L TAVERN

3207 N. Clark St. (3200N, 900W)
Chicago, IL 60657
(773) 528-1303

Website	None
Neighborhood	Lakeview
Open 'til & Cover	2am (3am Sat); never a cover
Drinks	Irish whiskey, bottled Pabst (no taps)
Food	Fuggedaboutit! (a good thing)
Music	An eclectic jukebox
Bar Type	Neighborhood Tavern, Dive Bar

Word has it that a bar has operated on this spot under various ownerships since 1934. Current proprietor Ken Frandsen has owned L&L Tavern for a decade and has preserved the name of his predecessors, Lefty & Loretta. Today, the L&L draws an intriguing cross-section of humanity, from neighborhood drunks to wayward Cub fans, in addition to a slew of nuevo-bohemian poseurs and employees after their shifts from nearby, legendary alternative clothiers, The Alley (3228 N. Clark) and Ragstock (812 W. Belmont). The notoriety that put L&L on the map came with being named "Best Dive" in Chicago in a *Stuff Magazine* write-up a few years ago. Those with a thirst for Irish whiskey will undoubtedly appreciate the 30 varieties available, ranging from the names you know like Jameson, Bushmill, and Tullamore Dew, to the lesser known like Murphy's, Red Breast, and Knappogue Castle. Though sunny by day and with a classic tin ceiling, L&L Tavern is quite dark in its native state and the regulars like it that way (when not outside for a smoke). You can also pull up a barstool at the ledge in front of the windows overlooking Clark, just as Jeffrey Dahmer did as he selected his next underage victim from the Dunkin Donuts across the street... While we're on the subject of serial killers, it is also said the John Gacy visited L&L at least once, donning his full, murderous clown costume.

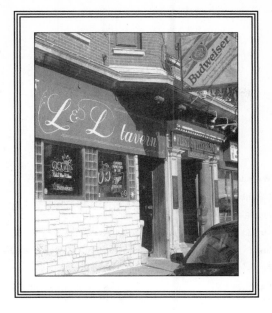

NEARBY	Spin Nightclub – 800 W. Belmont Ave. (gay)
	Johnny O'Hagan's – 3374 N. Clark St.
	Brew & View at the Vic – 3145 N. Sheffield Ave.
SIMILAR	**LEGENDARY DIVE BARS**
	Billy Goat Tavern – 430 N. Michigan Ave.
	Old Town Ale House – 219 W. North Ave.
	Weeds Tavern – 1555 N. Dayton St.
	IMPRESSIVE HARD LIQUOR SELECTIONS
	Duke of Perth – 2913 N. Clark St. (Scotch)
	Delilah's – 2771 N. Lincoln Ave. (bourbon)
	Salud – 1471 N. Milwaukee Ave. (tequila)
TRIVIA	Can you name the three remaining Irish distilleries?
NOTES	_____
	_____
	_____
	_____
	_____
	_____
	_____

ANSWER: *Bushmills, Middleton, and Cooley.*

LASCHET'S INN

2119 W. Irving Park Rd. (4000N, 2200W)
Chicago, IL 60618
(773) 478-7915

Website	www.laschetsinn.com
Neighborhood	North Center
Open 'til & Cover	2am (3am Sat); never a cover
Drinks	12 German beers, served up to 15 liters
Food	Schnitzel and other Teutonic delights
Music	Oompah, played at times by bartender
Bar Type	Neighborhood Tavern, Bierstube

Laschet's Inn opened back when many German immigrants inhabited Chicago's North Side. They have since moved, and their children and grandchildren have become less interested in the Old Country. However, a rather interesting trend has emerged in the last few years: new German pubs have opened—consider Glunz, Überstein, and Prost—and old standbys like Laschet's have experienced new life and clientele. Laschet's is well known for serving an excellent wiener-schnitzel, its imported libations, and for once-upon-a-time barkeep Karl Laschet, who opened his namesake pub in 1971. Laschet oversaw the festivities around Chicago's annual Von Steuben Day Parade of the German-American Fest (Oktoberfest) for many years, and is remembered with the honorary "Karl Laschet Avenue" that runs through the heart of Lincoln Square. In 1991, Franz and Ursula Kokott took over, and Ursula opened the kitchen in 2000 after years of frying up *frikadellen* (meat-loaf-like burgers) for patrons anyway. Matt and Mannie Lodge took the helm in 2007 and keep the place true to its roots, continuing to attract German regulars (authentically speaking German at the bar!), as well as younger residents and other visitors that get a kick out of the German "theme." Bonus: In the main bar hangs a mural depicting several rotund "angels" engaged in various degrees of debauchery with the words: *Wir kommen alle, alle in den Himmel...weil wir so brav sind!* In English: "We are all coming, all to Heaven... because we are so well-behaved!" Prost!

NEARBY	O'Donovan's – 2100 W. Irving Park Rd.
	Windy City Inn – 2257 W. Irving Park Rd.
	Chicago Joe's – 2256 W. Irving Park Rd.

NEARBY GERMANIC RESTAURANTS & TAVERNS

SIMILAR

Resi's Bierstube – 2034 W. Irving Park Rd.
Glunz Bavarian Haus – 4128 N. Lincoln Ave.
Chicago Brauhaus – 4732 N. Lincoln Ave.

INTRIGUING PUB MURAL & ARTWORK

Old Town Ale House – 219 W. North Ave.
Nick's Beergarden – 1516 N. Milwaukee Ave.
Simon's Tavern – 5210 N. Clark St.

TRIVIA   What does Laschet's black eagle logo stand for?

NOTES   _____

_____

_____

_____

_____

_____

_____

_____

ANSWER: *The coat of arms of Germany.*

LINCOLN TAVERN

1858 W. Wabansia Ave. (1700N, 1900W)
Chicago, IL 60622
(773) 342-7778

Website	www.lincolntavern.com
Neighborhood	Bucktown
Open 'til & Cover	2am (3am Sat); never a cover
Drinks	Handful of taps, love the PBR
Food	Roast duck (Friday), ribs, pork chops
Music	Jingles from commercials on WGN TV
Bar Type	Neighborhood Tavern, Restaurant

Deep in the heart of Bucktown lies a quiet Chicago institution that locals love for its lodge-like décor, weekly duck special (reserve one in advance), and a relaxed atmosphere that gets even more so the more Pabst Blue Ribbons you drink. The building housing Lincoln Tavern dates back to 1890. Community memory has it that a bar has operated out of the first floor since then, with a brief interlude as an ice cream parlor during Prohibition. Lincoln Tavern itself was established in 1934 and named after Lincoln Street, the north-south cross street until it was renamed "Wolcott Avenue" in the 1940s. Albert and Sophie Folak took ownership of the Lincoln Tavern in 1950, and the family has run the place ever since, with Bill Folak taking over in 1970 and his son, Bill Folak, Jr., now representing the third generation of ownership. While the glass block façade speaks to the Bohemian neighborhood surrounding it, the taxidermy, deer antler chandeliers, and hunting photos on the interior scream Wisconsin Northwoods. Step through what looks like the exterior of a log cabin, just beyond the main bar, and you'll find Lincoln Tavern's restaurant. This room was once an apartment of the original owners but now features a stone fireplace and fake windows that look out across a painted woodland scene, backlit to look like daylight. It may very well be the definition of cozy.

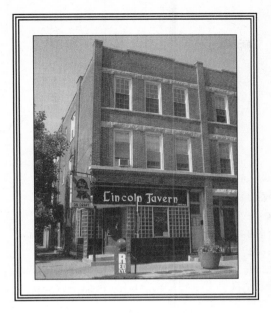

NEARBY   Club Lucky – 1824 W. Wabansia Ave.
Bucktown Pub – 1658 W. Cortland Ave.
Marie's Riptide Lounge – 1745 W. Armitage Ave.

SIMILAR   **WEST TOWN PROHIBITION-ERA TAVERNS**
Rainbo Club – 1150 N. Damen Ave.
Gold Star Bar – 1755 W. Division St.
Beachwood Inn – 1415 N. Wood St.
LODGE-LIKE PUBS
Will's Northwoods Inn – 3032 N. Racine Ave.
Huettenbar – 4721 N. Lincoln Ave.
The Lodge – 21 W. Division St.

TRIVIA   Uncommon for a bar, what does the Lincoln
Tavern sell that you would normally find in a
convenience store?

NOTES   _____

_____

_____

_____

_____

_____

LOCAL OPTION

1102 W. Webster Ave. (2200N, 1100W)
Chicago, IL 60614
(773) 348-2008

Website	None
Neighborhood	Lincoln Park
Open 'til & Cover	2am (3am Sat); never a cover
Drinks	Surprisingly varied beer selection
Food	New Orleans–style seafood
Music	Good juke when Cubs aren't playing
Bar Type	Neighborhood Tavern, Oyster Bar

Deep in the heart of Lincoln Park, in the Sheffield Neighbors enclave, is a captivating shack known as the Local Option to area residents, and students and professors from nearby DePaul University. Shortly after it opened in 1986, original owner Hugh Haller convinced the Rolling Rock brewery that there was a market for their beer in Chicago and he promised to decorate his pub with as much swag as they could provide. Lo and behold, Rolling Rock cracked the Chicago market and has sponsored the neighborhood's Sheffield Garden Walk street festival for many years. Their swag is gone since new ownership took over, but you can still get Rolling Rock in the bottle along with 25 microbrews and imports on tap that are likely to be new even to the most seasoned beer enthusiasts, a nice way to wash down the bar's Cajun offerings. All of this is a refreshing change from its predecessor, The Chessman, a rough biker bar known alternately as Fred & Tiny's. When Hugh Haller purchased the joint, area residents—who rued the day the Chessman opened—attempted to exercise their "local option." This term refers to a Chicago ordinance that allows neighborhoods to keep taverns out by voting their precincts dry. A rumor circulated that the new bar would be a gay punk rock club with a 1,000-foot outdoor deck. Fortunately, cooler heads prevailed and we can commemorate their victory today with a Rolling Rock, while pondering its mysterious "33."

NEARBY   Charlie's on Webster – 1224 W. Webster Ave.
Kelly's Pub – 949 W. Webster Ave.
McGee's – 950 W. Webster Ave.

SIMILAR   **NEIGHBORHOOD SEAFOOD**
Half Shell – 676 W. Diversey Pkwy.
King Crab Tavern – 1816 N. Halsted St.
Cy's Crab House – 3819 N. Ashland Ave.
**QUIET YET NOTABLE NEIGHBORHOOD
TAVERNS**
Cody's Public House – 1658 W. Barry Ave.
Four Moon Tavern – 1847 W. Roscoe St.
G&L Fire Escape – 2157 W. Grace St.

TRIVIA   Jambalaya (served at Local Option) is a New
World version of what Old World recipe?

NOTES   _____

_____

_____

_____

_____

_____

ANSWER: Spain's paella.

THE LODGE

21 W. Division St. (1200N, 0W)
Chicago, IL 60610
(312) 642-4406

Website	www.rushanddivision.com
Neighborhood	Gold Coast
Open 'til & Cover	4am (5am Sat); never a cover
Drinks	The usual, though more beer-heavy
Food	Peanuts with shells thrown on the floor
Music	Rat Pack on an old Wurlitzer jukebox
Bar Type	Meat Market, Late-Night

Self-described as, "hosting Chicago's longest cocktail hour," The Lodge is indeed the oldest and most notorious denizen of the crowded Rush & Division nightlife district in the Gold Coast neighborhood. It's also one of the smaller holdings of the Lodge Management empire that includes nearby Mother's (p. 130), Mothers Too, Bootleggers, She-nannigan's House of Beer, Pippin's, and Hangge Uppe (p. 84). Like its sibling bars, The Lodge is popular with conventioneers, tourists, and sub-urbanites, though even urban night owls get sucked in… The Lodge dates back to 1957, replacing a jazz club named Suzy's (originally Allegro). Former owner, Paul Risolia, renovated the tavern with its current ski lodge motif in 1962, and the rest is history. Upon entry, belly up to the ornately carved Dutch oak bar with shingled overhang, and grab yourself a bowl of com-plimentary peanuts as you await your cocktail. Older patrons are often found swing dancing to Ol' Blue Eyes, often in hopes of a brief, yet "special" encounter. A younger crowd, with sim-ilar intentions, gravitates towards the front windows to keep an eye on incoming talent, while wondering if they should have gone to the more raucous Finn McCool's across the alley instead. Beware: Cougar sightings are common.

NEARBY	Mother's, The Original – 26 W. Division St.
	Butch McGuire's – 21 W. Division St.
	She-nannigan's House of Beer –
	16 W. Division St.
SIMILAR	**OLDER, LATE-NIGHT CROWDS**
	Miller's Pub – 134 S. Wabash Ave.
	Burton Place – 1447 N. Wells St.
	Green Mill Cocktail Lounge –
	4802 N. Broadway
	LODGE-LIKE PUBS
	Will's Northwoods Inn – 3032 N. Racine Ave.
	Lincoln Tavern – 1858 W. Wabansia Ave.
	Huettenbar – 4721 N. Lincoln Ave.
TRIVIA	According to rumor, what former Cub frequented the Lodge and popularized the term "slump buster" (meaning to have *relations* with an ugly groupie in order to bust a batting slump)?
NOTES	_____
	_____
	_____
	_____

ANSWER: *Mark Grace.*

LOTTIE'S PUB

1858 W. Wabansia Ave. (1700N, 1900W)
Chicago, IL 60622
(773) 342-7778

Website	www.lottiespub.com
Neighborhood	Bucktown
Open 'til & Cover	2am (3am Sat); never a cover
Drinks	25 beers on tap, menu of 8 "bombs"
Food	The usual pub grub, crinkle-cut fries
Music	Jukebox
Bar Type	Neighborhood Tavern, Sports Bar

Set amongst alternative havens like Charleston, Danny's Tavern, and Gallery Cabaret, Lottie's Pub appears to be one of the few mainstream neighborhood sports bars in Bucktown, though Lottie's history tells a different story. Walter Zagorski who ran this corner pub as Zagorski's Tavern, acquired the building in 1934. Walter, standing 6' tall and with a deep voice, was a flamboyant transvestite and possible hermaphrodite, who preferred to go by "Lottie." Lottie was as infamous as "she" was colorful, running a gambling operation in the basement—"Zagorski's Rathskeller"—that featured such distractions as horse betting, poker games, and strippers. Access to the rathskeller was by a private door through which gangsters, area residents, and politicians alike were welcomed. Zagorski's was a favorite of novelist Nelson Algren, who lived six blocks south at 1958 W. Evergreen Avenue. Lottie was arrested as the leader of a bookmaking ring, following a joint crackdown by the FBI and IRS. After a subsequent grand jury testimony, she died of natural causes in 1973. Zagorski's closed and became a pub named Busia's in the 1980s. Bill Lockhart opened Lottie's Pub in 1986 to commemorate Zagorski, and now offers more beer on tap than most bars and sports on flat screens instead of bookmaking. Today at the bar, you can still find a photograph of a manly-looking Lottie in a lovely flower-print dress.

NEARBY	Lemming's on Damen – 1850 N. Damen Ave.
	Ed & Jean's – 2032 W. Armitage Ave.
	Bucktown Pub – 1658 W. Cortland Ave.
SIMILAR	**BUCKTOWN-WICKER PARK SPORTS BARS**
	Cans – 1640 N. Damen Ave.
	Aberdeen – 1856 W. North Ave.
	Boundary – 1932 W. Division St.
	OTHER NELSON ALGREN HAUNTS
	Tufano's – 1073 W. Vernon Park Pl.
	Gold Star Bar – 1755 W. Division St.
	Rainbo Club – 1150 N. Damen Ave.
TRIVIA	Whose bones were found here a few years ago?
NOTES	_____
	_____
	_____
	_____
	_____
	_____
	_____
	_____

ANSWER: A dog's; foul play was initially suspected.

MARGE'S STILL

1758 N. Sedgwick St. (1800N, 400W)
Chicago, IL 60614
(312) 664-9775

Website	www.margeschicago.com
Neighborhood	Old Town Triangle
Open 'til & Cover	2am (3am Sat); never a cover
Drinks	A handful of beers (six on tap), wine
Food	Upscale pub grub, kids menu, brunch
Music	Unremarkable jukebox
Bar Type	Neighborhood Tavern

Like evilOlive is our favorite bar palindrome, Marge's Still is our favorite double entendre. A still is used to make whiskey, and it's also a reference to the continuing legacy of previous owner Marge Lednick, who ran Marge's Pub since 1955. The building itself dates back to 1885 and operated as a speakeasy during Prohibition, with gin supplied from a bathtub upstairs. Marge passed away in 2001 and the place was bought two years later by Pam & Andreas Antoniou, who also run nearby Old Town Pub, Pepper Canister, and Garret Ripley's. After fighting the city for four years, the new owners finally obtained their elusive "incidental liquor license." The tavern was reopened in July 2007 and renamed Marge's Still to honor its former proprietor, and perhaps as a tongue-in-cheek jab at the city itself. As such, a Chicago landmark has been preserved and revitalized rather than becoming yet another condo building, as was the fate of now-defunct originals, Artful Dodger and Thurston's. The beautiful wooden bar, "bar bistro" fare, and sunny windows overlooking Sedgwick makes Marge's Still a far cry from its predecessor's walls of yellowed stucco, pinball machines, an upright piano once played by the blind Al Gray, and cockroach races on the battered wooden bar. Fortunately for us all, Marge's Still remains an unpretentious corner tavern that Marge herself would surely be proud of, still.

NEARBY   Twin Anchors – 1655 N. Sedgwick St.
Bricks – 1909 N. Lincoln Ave.
Sedgwick's – 1935 N. Sedgwick St.

SIMILAR   **OLDEST CHICAGO PUBS**
Schaller's Pump – 3714 S. Halsted St. (1881)
17 West at the Berghoff – 17 W. Adams St.
  (1898)
Green Mill – 4802 N. Broadway (1907)
GASTRONOMIC PUBS
The Gage – 24 S. Michigan Ave.
Silver Cloud – 1700 N. Damen Ave.
Mrs. Murphy & Sons – 3905 N. Lincoln Ave.

TRIVIA   What was Marge doing upon the author's only
encounter with her at Marge's Pub?

NOTES   _____

_____

_____

_____

_____

_____

ANSWER: *Smoking a joint at the end of the bar.*

Marie's Riptide Lounge

1750 W. Armitage Ave. (2000N, 1800W)
Chicago, IL 60647
(773) 278-7317

Website	None
Neighborhood	Bucktown
Open 'til & Cover	4am (5am Sat); never a cover
Drinks	Bottled beer, Jägermeister
Food	Bags of chips; beer is food…
Music	Jukebox Rat Pack, torchlight, oldies
Bar Type	Dive Bar, Late-Night

Like a tavern out of David Lynch's *Twin Peaks*, Marie's Riptide Lounge is a timeless gem that stands out even in a neighborhood filled with unique, charismatic bars. Named in honor of Hawaii becoming the 50th State, Marie's Riptide Lounge has inebriated an evolving, late-night clientele since 1961, when owner, Marie Wuczynski, opened the tavern that takes her name. As the rest of the name implies, a tiki theme was originally planned but polka and beer quickly replaced hula music and umbrella-topped cocktails. On the other hand, it's not unusual to find Marie sporting a Hawaiian shirt with her beehive white hair, dispensing magic tricks and wet willies… As the Polish clientele moved on, a younger crowd moved in, beginning with Bill Murray and John Belushi in the '70s (while away from Old Town Ale House, p. 148), and later Andy Richter, who brought *Late Night with Conan O'Brien* on a Chicago bar crawl in 1997 (after Resi's Bierstube, p. 160). Located at the "Meeting of the Ages" (Armitage and Hermitage avenues), and almost under the Kennedy Expressway, you'll find yourself transported to a bygone era when you step through the door, with Marie's diner-like interior and handful of Polish regulars who stop by early (and have been coming from day one). A sign of its far-reaching appeal, Marie's appears in an episode of the '80s TV show, *Crime Story*, and is the subject of songs by Robbie Fulks and Michael McDermott.

NEARBY	Bucktown Pub – 1658 W. Cortland St.
	Lincoln Tavern – 1858 W. Wabansia Ave.
	Club Lucky – 1824 W. Wabansia Ave.
SIMILAR	**TOP LATE-NIGHT BARS**
	Green Mill Cocktail Lounge –
	4802 N. Broadway
	Redhead Piano Bar – 16 W. Ontario St.
	Carol's Pub – 4659 N. Clark St.
	TOP BUCKTOWN BARS
	Hideout – 1354 W. Wabansia Ave.
	Map Room – 1949 N. Hoyne Ave.
	Charleston – 2076 N. Hoyne Ave.
TRIVIA	Hawaii was 1 of 4 states that were independent prior to joining the U.S. What are the other three?

NOTES _____

_____

_____

_____

_____

_____

ANSWER: *Texas, California, and Vermont.*

MATCHBOX

770 N. Milwaukee Ave. (800N, 1200W)
Chicago, IL 60622
(312) 666-9292

Website	None
Neighborhood	River West
Open 'til & Cover	2am (3am Sat); never a cover
Drinks	Bartenders skilled in the cocktail arts
Food	Eat in adjacent Silver Palm train car
Music	Whatever the bartenders play
Bar Type	Neighborhood Tavern

Much like the perennial Cajun favorite Heaven on Seven offers the most gumbo-per-square-foot in the city, Matchbox offers the most cocktails-per-square-foot as "Chicago's most intimate bar." The quasi-triangular, one-room building is actually the shape of a book of matches placed on its side. Some speculate that the original owner meant to call his place Matchbook but had a limited command of English. Current owner and restaurateur, David Gevercer of Gare St. Lazare and Bistro Europa, purchased Matchbox from an old Israeli named Siegel, who ran the place since World War II. Rather than knocking it down and expanding into the lot next door acquired as part of the sale, Gevercer preserved Matchbox's cozy atmosphere and re-opened in 1995. Gevercer went on to build a restaurant & bar in the adjacent lot around a 1947 Budd dining car that once ran along the Atlantic Coast Line Railroad, also known as *The Silver Palm*. As you push open the bar's door, please do so carefully as there's likely to be someone on the other side. A worn, candle-lit wooden bar spans almost the entire length of the southern wall and you'll literally have to squeeze your way past those sitting towards the end of it, as the space tapers even more narrowly as you head to the restrooms in back. The appeal of the Matchbox is that it is more intimate than small, and the art of conversation with friendly locals never disappoints.

NEARBY	Red Canary – 695 N. Milwaukee Ave.
	Emmit's Pub – 495 N. Milwaukee Ave.
	Paramount Room – 415 N. Milwaukee Ave.
SIMILAR	**SMALLEST CHICAGO PUBS**
	Zebra Lounge – 1220 N. State Pkwy.
	Dram Shop – 3040 N. Broadway
	Marty's Wine & Martini Bar –
	1511 W. Balmoral Ave.
	TRAIN THEME
	Tutto Italiano Ristorante – 501 S. Wells St.
	Fast Track (hot dog stand) – 629 W. Lake St.
	Blue Line Club Car – 1548 N. Damen Ave.
TRIVIA	Between which two cities did *The Silver Palm* run?
NOTES	

MILLER'S PUB

134 S. Wabash Ave. (200S, 100E)
Chicago, IL 60603
(312) M-I-L-L-E-R-S

Website	www.millerspub.com
Neighborhood	Loop
Open 'til & Cover	4am (5am Sat); never a cover
Drinks	Standard with drafts in a pint or stein
Food	Ribs, steaks, chops
Music	Steel on porcelain and din of the crowd
Bar Type	Neighborhood Tavern, Late-Night

Miller's Pub opened in 1935 by a pair of Irish brothers, making it the second oldest restaurant in Chicago behind nearby Berghoff. The pub was purchased by the somewhat less-than-Irish Gallios Brothers in 1948 and moved in 1989 from 23 W. Adams to its present location, formerly a furniture store, jeweler, and restaurant called Vannie's (after another Gallios Brother). Once a favorite of Jimmy Durante, Milton Berle, and George Burns, Miller's Pub attracts fewer celebrities today, as most prefer back doors and VIP rooms to avoid drunken YouTube moments. On the other hand, you can still find a classic, supper club–type menu with steaks, chops, and the best baby back ribs in the Loop. At the east end of the bar, you'll find an area marked Bill Veeck's Corner to honor long-time regular and Chicago sports legend Bill Veeck—the man who planted ivy on the walls at Wrigley Field, started fire-works displays and outfield showers at Comiskey Park, and sent dwarf Eddie Gaedel to the plate in 1958 (jersey number: 1/8). For visitors, Loop office denizens, and residents alike, Miller's Pub is easily one of the best downtown bars for lunch, post-work or pre-theatre, and for boisterous late-night action. And, in case you're wondering, the hobos in the paintings above the bar were once Miller's Pub regulars in the 1950s that allowed themselves to be painted by Art Institute students in exchange for the management pardoning their "tab."

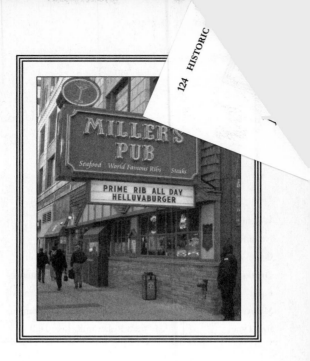

NEARBY	Exchequer Pub – 226 S. Wabash Ave.
	17 West at the Berghoff – 17 W. Adams St.
	The Gage – 24 S. Michigan Ave.
SIMILAR	**CELEBRITY HANGOUTS**
	Pump Room – 1301 N. State Pkwy.
	Green Mill Cocktail Lounge –
	4802 N. Broadway
	Kingston Mines – 2548 N. Halsted St.
	CLASSIC RIB JOINTS
	Twin Anchors – 1655 N. Sedgwick St.
	Fireplace Inn – 1448 N. Wells St.
	Fireside Restaurant – 5739 N. Ravenswood Ave.
TRIVIA	What celebrity came to Miller's when he wasn't having ribs at Twin Anchors?
NOTES	_____
	_____
	_____
	_____
	_____
	_____

ANSWER: *Frank Sinatra.*

MIRABELL RESTAURANT & LOUNGE

3454 W. Addison Ave. (3500W, 3600N)
Chicago, IL 60618
(773) 463-1962

Website	www.mirabellrestaurant.com
Neighborhood	Irving Park
Open 'til & Cover	2am (closed Sun); never a cover
Drinks	35 Teutonic brews served in steins
Food	Wienerschnitzel, infamous bean pot
Music	Both live and pre-recorded oompah
Bar Type	Austrian Restaurant, Beer Hall

For those Cub fans and Old Irving Park neighbors wondering what goes on in the building with the *Fachwerk* façade (faux timber–framed, with criss-crossing beams) across from the K-Mart at St. Louis Avenue, it's Mirabell: an Austrian restaurant and beer garden. Mirabell opened in 1967, the handiwork of Hans and Katherine Dobler, who named the place after Mirabell Gardens in Salzburg, Austria (Katherine's hometown). There originally was a glass room to the left of the bar with a tree growing through it, a space that now features coats of arms, commemorative plates, Bavarian murals, and enough taxidermy to make the owners of Will's Northwoods Inn jealous. Access to the beer garden is through the western wall. Present owners Werner and Anita Heil purchased Mirabell in 1977. Werner worked as a chef at the Golden Ox, the now-defunct German restaurant that was as loved as the dearly departed Zum Deutschen Eck, Heidelberger Fass, and Metro Club. Werner now offers a full menu of Old World classics served by stout older women brought over from the Old Country. Heil was also the first to import BBK beer from Germany, an acronym for Barbarossa-Bräu Kaiserslautern. History buffs may be interested to know that BBK is never referred to by its whole name, not because of length, but instead because Barbarossa was the code name for Hitler's invasion of Russia. *Herzlich Wilkommen!*

NEARBY   Abbey Pub – 3420 W. Grace St.
Chief O'Neill's Pub – 3471 N. Elston Ave.
ñ – 2977 N. Elston Ave.

SIMILAR   **NEARBY GERMAN RESTAURANTS & TAVERNS**
Laschet's Inn – 2119 W. Irving Park Rd.
Chicago Brauhaus – 4732 N. Lincoln Ave.
Lutz Continental Café – 2458 W. Montrose Ave.
MORE TAXIDERMY
Will's Northwoods Inn – 3032 N. Racine Ave.
Lincoln Tavern – 1858 W. Wabansia Ave.
Mecca Supper Club – 6666 N. Northwest Hwy.

TRIVIA   What famous cartoonist (retired) painted the
murals at Mirabell?

NOTES   _____

_____

_____

_____

_____

_____

_____

ANSWER: Gary Larson of "The Far Side."

MONK'S PUB

205 W. Lake St. (200N, 20W)
Chicago, IL 60606
(312) 357-6665

Website	www.mmonks.com
Neighborhood	Loop
Open 'til & Cover	2am (closed Sat/Sun); never a cover
Drinks	6 tap beers & 6 wines by the glass
Food	Half-pound burgers, chili, free peanuts
Music	Good tunes on a Wurlitzer jukebox
Bar Type	Dive Bar, After-Work

Monk's Pub dates back to 1969 when it was a subterranean hole-in-the-wall on Lower Wacker Drive. The pub moved to its current spot in 1971 after the original was demolished. The current owner took over in May 1978 and has remodeled the pub to reflect the monastery where he resided one summer as a boy. The exterior of Monk's Pub looks like a European inn with its kerosene lanterns and wooden sign, handmade in Barcelona. Thick wooden doors separate the hectic downtown hullabaloo and rumble of the Loop "L" trains overhead from an interior adorned with exposed brick walls and wooden barrels. The antique Tiffany-like Schlitz lanterns hanging over the bar were given to the pub by the distributor in recognition of it being the first beer featured on tap at Monk's. The pub is most popular at lunch and after work when ties are discarded as quickly as the first peanut shells hit the floor, both of which are strongly encouraged. As you would guess, the pub draws Loop office workers, traders straying north from Cactus Bar & Grill (motto: "Don't drink and trade"), and lawyers that have argued more cases in Monk's than at nearby Cook County courthouse. Bookworms appreciate the small library of leather-bound books in the rear, but may find that patrons tend to take the opposite of a vow of silence and any thoughts of serious reading are quickly discarded for another ale.

NEARBY   Sidebar Grille – 221 N. LaSalle St.
Cardozo's Pub – 170 W. Washington St.
Coogan's Riverside Saloon – 180 N. Wacker Dr.

SIMILAR   **MONK REFUGES**
Friar Tuck – 3010 N. Broadway
Moody's Pub – 5910 N. Broadway
Hopleaf Bar – 5148 N. Clark St.

OLD EUROPE
Huettenbar – 4721 N. Lincoln Ave.
Mirabell Restaurant & Lounge –
3454 W. Addison
Fadó – 100 W. Grand Ave.

TRIVIA   In what neighborhood is Chicago's Monastery
of the Holy Cross also serving as a bed &
breakfast?

NOTES   _____

_____

_____

_____

_____

_____

ANSWER: *Bridgeport, at 31st & Aberdeen.*

MOODY'S PUB

5910 N. Broadway (5900N, 1200W)
Chicago, IL 60660
(773) 275-2696

Website	www.moodyspub.com
Neighborhood	Edgewater
Open 'til & Cover	2am (3am Sat); never a cover
Drinks	Steins of Berghoff Ale
Food	Heavenly "Moody Bleu" (all you need)
Music	Seasonal: swallows or roaring fireplace
Bar Type	Neighborhood Tavern

Moody's Pub is one of the best Chicago bars that many non-locals have never heard of, mainly because of its far north location in Edgewater. Moody's Pub is certainly worth the trip as it's tough to beat for its burgers, beer garden in summer, fireplace in winter, and relaxed atmosphere all year 'round. What has been an Edgewater institution since 1967 actually began much further south. Moody's Pub first opened in 1959 on North Avenue in Old Town by John Moody and Ray Zago, when Old Town was transitioning from Old World Europe into a West Coast–inspired Bohemia, and one of the city's top tourist destinations. This was due to the carnival atmosphere of Wells Street and Piper's Alley created by a plentitude of new shops, bars, and restaurants. Following the urban facelift of Old Town in the late '60s, Moody and Zago moved their beloved joint to the site of a former used car lot on Broadway, with an apartment for Moody's family on the second floor. The multilevel beer garden, filled with silver oak trees, waterfalls, and french fry–bandit swallows, harkens back to the beer garden found at the original Moody's. Everyone, particularly students from Loyola University about a mile north, can appreciate burgers for under $7, pitchers for under $10, and a list of intriguing cocktail creations (served both hot and cold) for under $6. In a world of $20 Kobe beef burgers and $15 martinis closer to the Loop, Moody's Pub delivers for both economical and metaphysical gain.

NEARBY	Ole St. Andrew's Inn – 5938 N. Broadway
	Pumping Company – 6157 N. Broadway
	Hamilton's Bar & Brill – 6341 N. Broadway
SIMILAR	**TOP BEER GARDENS**
	Castaways – 1603 N. Lakeshore Dr.
	John Barleycorn Memorial Pub –
	658 W. Belden Ave.
	Sheffield's – 3258 N. Sheffield Ave.
	FIREPLACE PUBS
	Fireplace Inn – 1448 N. Wells St.
	Duffy's Tavern – 420 1/2 W. Diversey Pkwy.
	Friar Tuck – 3010 N. Broadway
TRIVIA	What was the first type of bleu cheese?
NOTES	_____
	_____
	_____
	_____
	_____
	_____
	_____

ANSWER: *Gorgonzola, dating back to 879 AD.*

MOTHER'S, THE ORIGINAL

26 W. Division St. (1200N, 0W)
Chicago, IL 60610
(312) 642-7251

Website	www.rushanddivision.com
Neighborhood	Gold Coast
Open 'til & Cover	3am (4am Sat), $5 cover on weekends
Drinks	The usual suspects
Food	Just olives and maraschino cherries
Music	DJ-spun dance music
Bar Type	Meat Market, Late-Night

One can only conclude that the name of this legendary singles joint is tongue-in-cheek…if your mother knew what you did here, she wouldn't sleep at night. The heart depicted in the Mother's logo reveals the truth: most coming to Mother's are looking for love—at least for one night—especially those making their way from the suburbs or out-of-town to relive scenes from *About Last Night* with Rob Lowe and Demi Moore, shot in part here. It has been this way since they first opened their doors in 1968. Descend into the subterranean depths and you will find two pool tables and DJ-spun karaoke in the front room, and Division Street's oldest and largest dance floor in the rear. In Spring Break fashion, this is the site of wet T-shirt, Mr. & Mrs. Division Street, and lip sync contests, as well as film screenings for independent Chicago filmmakers. The present ownership of Lodge Management Group claims that such bands as *Cream*, *Velvet Underground*, *Chicago*, and *The Mekons* once played in the back room, though today this success is unlikely to be replicated as the space features live band karaoke on Thursday nights, an occasional cover band on Saturday nights, and DJs every other night. This location is known as The Original Mother's because you'll find Mother's Too a few doors down, operating as an above-ground sports bar (and weekend meat market) by the same owners.

NEARBY	Butch McGuire's – 20 W. Division St. (next door)
	The Lodge – 21 W. Division St.
	Mother's Too – 14 W. Division St.
SIMILAR	**OTHER 1968 TAVERNS**
	Kingston Mines – 2548 N. Halsted St.
	Four Farthings – 2060 N. Cleveland Ave.
	Wise Fools Pub – 2270 N. Lincoln Ave.
	KARAOKEVILLE
	Trader Todd's – 3216 N. Sheffield Ave.
	Excalibur Nightclub – 632 N. Dearborn St.
	Hidden Cove – 5336 N. Lincoln Ave.
TRIVIA	What other classic Chicago tavern was filmed in *About Last Night*?

NOTES

_____

_____

_____

_____

_____

_____

_____

_____

ANSWER: *Kelly's Pub in Lincoln Park.*

MURPHY'S BLEACHERS

3655 N. Sheffield Ave. (3700N, 1000W)
Chicago, IL 60613
(773) 281-3685

Website	www.murphysbleachers.com
Neighborhood	Wrigleyville
Open 'til & Cover	2am (3am Sat); never a cover
Drinks	The finest Old Style, served in cans
Food	Ballpark-style burgers, hotdogs, brats
Music	*Go, Cubs, Go!* by Steve Goodman
Bar Type	Sports Bar

Just beyond the friendly confines of Wrigley Field is *the* place to go before and after Cub games for fans and players alike. Former NIU grad and Chicago police officer, Jim Murphy, purchased the bar in 1980, applied his surname to the shingle, and developed it into the most popular beer garden in Wrigleyville. Previously, the place was a dive bar known as Ray's Bleacher's, opened by Ray Meyer in 1965—and no, not the DePaul coach of the same name. Ray's served as the ancestral home of the original Left Field Bleacher Bums, a "seemingly" unemployed group of miscreants led by Rob Grousl, who began the tradition of throwing back opponents' home runs. Prior to that, the place was JB's Bleachers, and before that, it was a drive up hot dog stand-turned-tavern named Ernie's Bleacher's that sold beer by the bucket following Prohibition. For maintaining and expanding a true Wrigleyville classic, you can thank Jim Murphy by having a beer in his memory. Jim lost the battle against liver cancer in 2003 at the age of 54. In addition to his Sheffield Avenue pride and joy, his work lives on at Mrs. Murphy's Irish Bistro (3905 N. Lincoln), a pub crafted out of a 1920s funeral home and fitted with a teak bar from County Wexford in Ireland and windows from the dearly departed German beer hall, Zum Deutschen Eck. Mrs. Murphy's, named after his wife Beth, was the last brainchild of Mr. Murphy. I'm sure that he can rest easy in knowing that the Cubs will win it all, maybe next year... Doh!

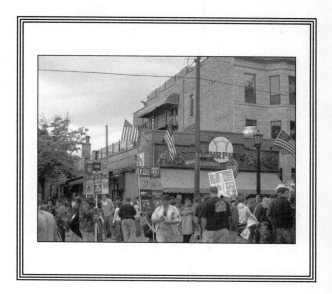

NEARBY	Casey Moran's – 3660–3662 N. Clark St.
	Harry Caray's Tavern – 3551 N. Sheffield Ave.
	The Dugout – 950 W. Addison St.
SIMILAR	**POST-GAME BEER GARDENS**
	Yak-zies on Clark – 3710 N. Clark St.
	Bernie's Tavern – 3664 N. Clark St.
	Vines on Clark – 3554 N. Clark St.
	NON-SPORTING WRIGLEYVILLE INSTITUTIONS
	Gingerman Tavern – 3740 N. Clark St.
	Nisei Lounge – 3439 N. Sheffield Ave.
	Guthries Tavern – 1300 W. Addison St.
TRIVIA	What was the first official name of Wrigley Field?
NOTES	_____
	_____
	_____
	_____
	_____
	_____
	_____

ANSWER: *Weeghman Park.*

THE MUTINY

2428 N. Western Ave. (2400N, 2400W)
Chicago, IL 60647
(773) 486-7774

Website	www.themutinychicago.com
Neighborhood	Logan Square
Open 'til & Cover	2am (3am Sat); never a cover
Drinks	Frosted 32-oz. mugs of Old Style, PBR
Food	None, Sonny's Pizza across the street
Music	Punk, Saturday afternoon karaoke
Bar Type	Dive Bar, Music Venue

This single-story, one-room building dates back 100 years, as evidenced by the famous men's room urinal. Not much is known about the heritage until a former journeyman boxer named Tommy Kluth ran it from the early '50s to May 1973. Back then, the draw at "Tommy Kluth's Gallery Bar-Headquarters, Veteran Boxers Association of Illinois, Ring No. 2" was a small boxing ring in the front of the bar, where Kluth would box patrons, though more for show than actual matches. Locals say the place was a two-lane bowling alley prior to that and a string of dive bars afterwards. The current owner, Ed, opened "The Mutiny Corporation" in September 1990 as part of his own rebellious act. Whatever his unspoken reason, Ed's Mutiny is our gain: free shows (no cabaret license) of the most raucous indie punk music around are held almost every day and also emanates from the jukebox. After early experiments and a watershed concert on Halloween 1998, by the *Gaza Strippers*, *The Nerves*, and *Grand Theft Auto*, the Mutiny has become *the* place for bands to cut their teeth, often being their first show or tour. Many bands will cause more than a few of your cilia to perish, but some acts just might make it big some day. In the meantime, you can always enjoy your 32-ounce Pabst Blue Ribbon while gazing at the full suit of armor and drop ceiling panels painted by regulars and local artists, à la Guthries Tavern (p. 78).

NEARBY	Quenchers Saloon – 2401 N. Western Ave.
	Bob Inn – 2609 W. Fullerton Ave.
	Fireside Bowl – 2648 W. Fullerton Ave.
SIMILAR	**INDIE MUSIC HAVENS**
	Empty Bottle – 1035 N. Western Ave.
	(indie rock)
	Hideout – 1354 W. Wabansia Ave. (indie folk)
	Phyllis' Musical Inn – 1800 W. Division St.
	CLASSIC DIVE BARS
	L&L Tavern – 3207 N. Clark St.
	Rainbo Club – 1150 N. Damen Ave.
	Gold Star Bar – 1755 W. Division St.
TRIVIA	Mutiny is reminiscent of what beloved Lincoln Park indie dive bar/rock club that closed in 2000?
NOTES	

_____

_____

_____

_____

_____

_____

_____

ANSWER: *Lounge Ax (2438 N. Lincoln).*

NEO

2350 N. Clark St. (2400N, 500W)
Chicago, IL 60614
(773) 528-2622

Website	www.neo-chicago.com
Neighborhood	Lincoln Park
Open 'til & Cover	8pm–4am (5am Sat); $5 Thu–Sat
Drinks	The usual, plus Chimay on tap
Food	"For the Soul" if you like the music
Music	Rotating New Wave, Gothic, Industrial
Bar Type	Nightclub, Late-Night

Chicago's oldest nightclub is as unlikely as its location: Down an alley between boutique shops is the dark and naughty Neo. The trio of Larry Acciari, Eric Larson, and Suzanne Shelton opened Neo on July 25, 1979, replacing a disco called "Hoots." Originally conceived as a punk bar, Neo quickly transitioned to New Wave and Shelton came up with the post-punk Gothic nightclub concept that you'll find today. Neo became so popular that it drew the likes of David Bowie, Iggy Pop, David Byrne, and U2. Big Time Productions bought Neo in 1982 and would later open the internationally syndicated nightclub Crobar as well as design Exit, Frank's, and the now-defunct Tequila Roadhouse. Neo has featured various looks over the years, including abstract artwork, art deco lighting, and a shark tank, but Big Time settled on Jordan Mozer's version of "Lower Wacker Drive" in 1988: thick concrete arches and columns, an 8,000-lb. concrete and terrazzo bar, and mirrors symbolizing the Chicago River. As popular as ever, diverse patrons wear any color as long as it's black, with extra credit for leather, odd facial hair, extra zippers, and unusual dance floor expression—though "normal" types also have a blast without worrying how they look. Like Ministry sang, every day is Halloween at Neo. While the beloved Gothic "Nocturna" Tuesdays are gone, other nights highlight metal, alternative, electronica, industrial, EBM, and the real crowd-pleaser: '80s Thursday nights.

NEARBY   The Other Side – 2436 N. Clark St.
Galway Arms – 2442 N. Clark St.
Mickey's – 2450 N. Clark St.

SIMILAR   **SO DARK... MWAHAHAHA!**
Exit – 1315 W. North Ave.
Liar's Club – 1665 W. Fullerton Ave.
Smart Bar – 3730 N. Clark St.
DARWINIAN NIGHTCLUBS
Hangge Uppe – 14 W. Elm St.
Excalibur Nightclub – 632 N. Dearborn St.
Crobar – 1512 N. Fremont St.

TRIVIA   Neo inspired which fictional character?

NOTES   _____

_____

_____

_____

_____

_____

_____

_____

ANSWER: The Matrix's Neo, by the local Wachowski brothers.

NEW APARTMENT LOUNGE

504 E. 75th St. (7500S, 500E)
Chicago, IL 60619
(773) 483-7728

Website	None
Neighborhood	Park Manor
Open 'til & Cover	4am (5am Sat); no cover (cash only)
Drinks	Cheap bottled beer and booze
Food	Nearby Army & Lou's BBQ before
Music	Von Freeman plays live on Tue night
Bar Type	Jazz Club, Neighborhood Tavern

The New Apartment Lounge opened in 1970 and is characteristic of most other dive bars in Chicago, known only to its locals and likely to stay that way. However, when the octogenarian Von Freeman plays saxophone on Tuesday nights, the New Apartment Lounge ditches its divey status and is elevated to one of the city's top jazz clubs. Born Earl Lavon Freeman on the South Side, Vonski's career began as a result of the Great Lakes Experience, an attempt to desegregate the Navy by recruiting black musicians at the Great Lakes Naval Training Center during World War II as morale boosters. This concentrated some of the best jazz talent in the country and produced such notable jazzmen as Freeman and Clark Terry. Having played with Lester Young, Coleman Hawkins, and Charlie Parker, Freeman may have been more renowned but he only plays in Chicago, having kept his regular gig at the New Apartment Lounge for almost 40 years. His "Express Yourself" jazz sessions begin at 10:30pm, though you'll want to get there an hour before to get a seat. The normally African-American crowd becomes more diverse on Vonski nights due to those coming from far and wide to hear his music, including younger musicians who hope to be invited onstage to play. In honor of his jazz career, the City of Chicago named this section of 75th Street, Honorary Von Freeman Way. No cover is charged but there is a two-drink minimum at the bar.

NEARBY	Lee's Unleaded Blues –
	7401 S. South Chicago Ave.
	50 Yard Line Bar & Grille – 69 E. 75th St.
	President's Lounge – 653 E. 75th St.
SIMILAR	**OTHER NOTABLE JAZZ CLUBS**
	Pops for Champagne – 601 N. State St.
	BackRoom – 1007 N. Rush St.
	Katerina's – 1920 W. Irving Park Rd.
	NOMADIC CHICAGO MUSIC INSTITUTIONS
	Jazz Showcase – 806 S. Plymouth Ct.
	New Velvet Lounge – 67 E. Cermak Rd.
	New Checkerboard Lounge – 5201 S. Harper Ct.
TRIVIA	With whom did Von Freeman record three albums?
NOTES	_____
	_____
	_____
	_____
	_____
	_____

NEW CHECKERBOARD LOUNGE

5201 S. Harper Ct. (5200S, 1500E)
Chicago, IL 60615
(773) 684-1472

Website	www.checkerboardhydepark.com
Neighborhood	Hyde Park
Open 'til & Cover	2am daily; $10–20 cover
Drinks	No taps, domestic beer, whiskey
Food	Order from nearby Dixie Kitchen
Music	Live blues & jazz nightly
Bar Type	Blues Club

What happens when the self-proclaimed Home of the Blues becomes homeless? Opened in 1972 by Buddy Guy, the Checkerboard Lounge at 423 E. 43d Street in Bronzeville played host to B.B. King, Magic Slim, Howlin' Wolf, Junior Wells, Chuck Berry, Eric Clapton, Rolling Stones, and Robert Plant—for starters. In addition to local regulars, the Checkerboard attracted University of Chicago students and European tourists, who would pay $8 for a guy on the street to watch their cars. The interior was run-down, but people loved the music, Aretha's Corner (named after a waitress), and a guy that regularly dressed up as the Lone Ranger. When the city shut down the bar in April 2003 for building code violations, blues lovers lamented its demise. Fortunately, U of C made a deal with current proprietor L.C. Thurman and the club re-opened over two years later, in the old Women's Workout World in the Harper Court Shopping Center. Today, a ramp leads up to the New Checkerboard Lounge, a more spacious and comfortable incarnation. Bands play on a checkerboard stage, observed by photos of Muddy Waters and Billie Holliday. Jazz and blues alternate during the week with bands starting at 9:30pm-ish and later on Saturdays. Sunday nights feature CheckerJAZZ, hosted by the Hyde Park Jazz Society from 7:30pm to 11:30pm. With no website or posted schedule, you'll just have to stop by to see who's playing, and it will likely be worth the trip.

NEARBY   Falcon Inn – 1601 E. 53rd St.
           Cove Lounge – 1750 E. 55th St.
           Jimmy's Woodlawn Tap – 1172 E. 55th St.
SIMILAR   SOUTH SIDE BLUES
           Buddy Guy's Legends – 754 S. Wabash Ave.
           Lee's Unleaded Blues –
              7401 S. South Chicago Ave.
           Linda's Place – 9823 S. Commercial Ave.
           NORTH SIDE BLUES
           B.L.U.E.S. – 2548 N. Halsted St.
           Kingston Mines – 2548 N. Halsted St.
           Rosa's Lounge – 3420 W. Armitage Ave.
TRIVIA   What former Checkerboard performer was also
           known as "The Queen of the Blues"?

NOTES   _____

           _____

           _____

           _____

           _____

           _____

ANSWER: Koko Taylor.

NEW VELVET LOUNGE

67 E. Cermak Rd. (2200S, 100E)
Chicago, IL 60616
(312) 791-9050

Website	www.velvetlounge.net
Neighborhood	South Loop
Open 'til & Cover	2am (3am Sat); $10–25 cover (cash)
Drinks	The usual suspects
Food	Only if you can eat jazz
Music	Live bebop and free-form jazz fusion
Bar Type	Jazz Club, Cocktail Lounge

There's a distinct absence of real velvet here—the smooth-ness of the Velvet Lounge comes instead from tenor sax man and owner, Fred Anderson, also an Arts Midwest Jazz Master and former Sun Ra band member. Anderson once ran a non-profit club in the mid-70s called Birdhouse (4512 N. Lincoln), named after Charlie "Bird" Parker. He later tended bar at Tip's Lounge on South Indiana to help out a sick friend. When the owner passed away, Fred took over and re-christened it Velvet Lounge in 1982. (The lounge was across from the Lexington Hotel where Geraldo Rivera in 1986 raided Al Capone's "secret vault," finding only dust and a bewildered cockroach inside.) When the building was sold for condo development, Anderson opened the New Velvet Lounge a few blocks south in 2006 with the help of a crew of dedicated volunteers/fans. Fortunately, the memorable chandeliers also moved and jazz continues nightly Wed–Sat. Bands start around 9pm and often feature Anderson himself playing alongside AACM—Association for the Advancement of Creative Musicians—members, a group of South Side jazz pioneers he co-founded in 1965. Sunday nights feature the Velvet Jam from 6:30pm until almost midnight ($5 cover). The audience is a combination of black South Siders, old-school jazz lovers, local music students, and adventurous North Siders. The common bond: everyone loves the jazz (and Fred).

NEARBY	Reggie's – 2105–9 S. State St.
	M Lounge – 1520 S. Wabash St.
	The Shrine – 2109 S. Wabash Ave.
SIMILAR	**OTHER NOTABLE JAZZ CLUBS**
	Green Mill Cocktail Lounge –
	4802 N. Broadway
	Andy's Jazz Club – 11 E. Hubbard St.
	BackRoom – 1007 N. Rush St.
	NOMADIC CHICAGO MUSIC INSTITUTIONS
	Jazz Showcase – 806 S. Plymouth Ct.
	New Apartment Lounge – 504 E. 75th St.
	New Checkerboard Lounge – 5201 S. Harper Ct.
TRIVIA	In what club did Anderson hear Charlie Parker's last Chicago performance?
NOTES	_____
	_____
	_____
	_____
	_____
	_____

NICK'S BEERGARDEN

1516 N. Milwaukee Ave. (1500N, 2000W)
Chicago, IL 60622
(773) 252-1155

Website	www.nicksbeergarden.com
Neighborhood	Wicker Park
Open 'til & Cover	4am (5am Sat); never a cover
Drinks	The usual, harder to get after 2am
Food	Only if you count the logo's pineapple
Music	Live w/e R&B, cool juke (now internet)
Bar Type	Dive Bar, Late-Night

Nick's Beergarden is well known for its eclectic outdoor patio and 4am liquor license, but less so for its storied past. Nick's originally opened in 1977, replacing a small bar and package liquor store that also served as a heroin shooting gallery at Halsted & Armitage where the Marquee Lounge is found today. Back then, Lincoln Park was seedy and Nick's was one of the first neighborhood taverns to cater to a younger crowd, including Caroline Kennedy, Artis Gilmore of the Bulls, and Ivan Dejesus of the Cubs. The décor was quasi-tropical with plastic pineapples, a stuffed sailfish, and a vintage surfboard. A large oil painting of a voluptuous nude officially known as Peaches, which some called Our Lady of Halsted Street, hung above the bar. In 1978, a man shot at Peaches four times with a .45, leaving three bullet holes in the painting and one in the frame. Fortunately, Peaches herself was spared injury. Nick's and its eccentric ornamentation moved in 1994 to its present Wicker Park locale, once the original location of the dear-departed Artful Dodger and the punk nightclub, Club Dreamerz. Nick's also features a pool table, its namesake beer garden (under the Blue Line "L"), and R&B bands every Friday (9pm) and Saturday (10pm) until the late-night crowd starts rolling in after midnight. As with the original, Nick's is owned by former schoolteacher, Nick Novich, who also runs Flat Iron across the street (once The Note), Nick's Uptown, and Nick's on Wilson.

NEARBY   Pint – 1547 N. Milwaukee Ave.
Rodan – 1530 N. Milwaukee Ave.
Violet Hour – 1520 N. Damen Ave.

SIMILAR   **WICKER PARK LATE-NIGHT**
Flat Iron – 1565 N. Milwaukee Ave.
Estelle's – 2013 W. North Ave.
Wicker Park Tavern – 1958 W. North Ave.
TOP WICKER PARK BARS
Double Door – 1572 N. Milwaukee Ave.
Piece – 1927 W. North Ave.
Silver Cloud – 1700 N. Damen Ave.

TRIVIA   The Artful Dodger appears in what Dickens
novel?

NOTES   _____

_____

_____

_____

_____

_____

_____

ANSWER: Oliver Twist.

NISEI LOUNGE

3439 N. Sheffield Ave. (3500N, 1000W)
Chicago IL, 60657
(773) 525-0557

Website	None
Neighborhood	Wrigleyville
Open 'til & Cover	2am (3am Sat); never a cover
Drinks	30 bottled bars including Asahi
Food	None, Matsuya around corner for sushi
Music	A jukebox-like, on-demand WXRT
Bar Type	Neighborhood Tavern, Japanese Pub

An island in a sea of sports bars, the Nisei Lounge is a Wrigleyville oddity: a quiet neighborhood bar with a unique character. With every bar in a three-block radius bursting at the seams with drunken fans after a Cubs game, it's as though Nisei resides in a parallel universe, unnoticed or forgotten as dust drifts in the rays of sunlight occasionally breaking through the tinted appliqué on the picture windows. The bar was named for the *Nisei*, or "lost generation" of American-born children of Japanese immigrants (the *Isei*). During World War II, almost all of these American citizens were imprisoned in Japanese internment camps. Once released, many Isei moved to Chicago, numbering 20,000 by the mid-1950s, second only in the U.S. to New York City. Today, the Nisei Lounge is a reminder that it wasn't too long ago that Japanese Americans were viewed with scrutiny, and this was one of the only places where they could congregate safely in public. The tavern first opened at Clark and Division in 1950 by Kaunch Hirabayashi and moved to its present location in 1958. Scott Martin, owner of Andersonville legend, Simon's Tavern (p. 176), along with Green Mill (p. 76) owner Dave Jemilo, purchased the Nisei Lounge in 1992. While the Japanese-American clientele has passed on, the lounge continues to honor the Nisei with Asahi Super Dry (the best-selling beer in Japan), a few Japanese covers on the jukebox, and by keeping the name, Nisei Lounge. *Kanpai!*

NEARBY   The Yard – 3441 N. Sheffield Ave.
               Dark Horse Tap & Grill – 3443 N. Sheffield Ave.
               Underground Lounge – 952 W. Newport Ave.

SIMILAR   **NON–WEST SIDE BOHEMIA**
               Hungry Brain – 2319 W. Belmont Ave.
               Ten Cat – 3931 N. Ashland Ave.
               Leadway Bar & Grill – 5233 N. Damen Ave.
               CLASSIC WRIGLEYVILLE TAVERNS
               Guthries Tavern – 1300 W. Addison St.
               Gingerman – 3740 N. Clark St.
               L&L Tavern – 3207 N. Clark St.

TRIVIA   In what year did Emperor Hirohito visit
               Chicago?

NOTES   _____

               _____

               _____

               _____

               _____

               _____

               _____

ANSWER: 1975.

OLD TOWN ALE HOUSE

219 W. North Ave. (1600N, 200W)
Chicago, IL 60610
(312) 944-7020

Website	www.oldtownalehouse.net
Neighborhood	Old Town
Open 'til & Cover	4am (5am Sat); never a cover
Drinks	Ale and "no blender or credit cards"
Food	Bags of potato chips & Milkbones
Music	Jazz-only jukebox
Bar Type	Neighborhood Tavern, Late-Night

When other bars close, neighborhood locals and celebrities alike head over to "Le Premiere Dive Bar," a.k.a., the Old Town Ale House. The present location is the second for this venerable institution, the first having opened across the street in 1958 as the bohemian Van Gelder's Ale House by Ed Van Gelder, who later opened John Barleycorn (p. 94). Former Figaro's bartender Arthur Klug and his wife Beatrice purchased the pub in 1971, but the bar caught fire shortly thereafter. The original bar and remaining furniture were quickly shuffled across the street to its current address in a "temporary" move lasting to this day. Because of its proximity to The Second City, Old Town Ale House has been popular with its comedians (John Belushi, Bill Murray, George Wendt, Chris Farley, et. al.), as well as other local celebrities (Nelson Algren, Mike Royko, Roger Ebert). Over 100 portraits of these and lesser-known regulars adorn the walls, including those honored on the northwest corner's "Dead Wall," kitty corner from "Crazy Bitch Wall." The painter is long-time regular Bruce Elliott, who along with his wife and Ale House bookkeeper, Tobin Mitchell, inherited the pub from Beatrice Klug who passed on eight months after Arthur in 2005. Many characters are still found at the Old Town Ale House today, all of whom share a common belief: that the liver is evil and must be punished.

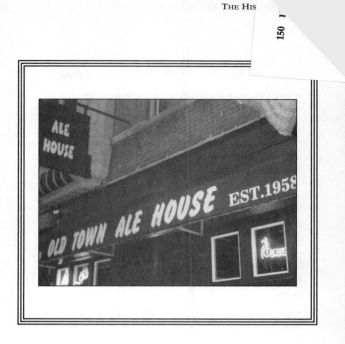

NEARBY	McGinny's Tap – 313 W. North Ave.
	Corcoran's Grill & Pub – 1615 N. Wells St.
	Wells on Wells – 1617 N. Wells St.
SIMILAR	**CELEBRITY HANGOUTS**
	Miller's Pub – 134 S. Wabash Ave.
	Pump Room – 1301 N. State Pkwy.
	Green Mill Cocktail Lounge –
	4802 N. Broadway
	CLASSIC LATE-NIGHT DIVES
	Mother's, The Original – 20 W. Division St.
	Marie's Riptide Lounge – 1750 W. Armitage Ave.
	Carol's Pub – 4659 N. Clark St.
TRIVIA	What long-running daytime program can always be found on TV at the Old Town Ale House?

NOTES _____

_____

_____

_____

_____

_____

ANSWER: *Jeopardy! at 3:30pm.*

PHYLLIS' MUSICAL INN

1800 W. Division St. (1200N, 1800W)
Chicago, IL 60622
(773) 486-9862

Website	None
Neighborhood	Ukrainian Village
Open 'til & Cover	2am (3am Sat); under $10 (if any)
Drinks	Cheap beer, highlighted by Old Style
Food	None, BBQ at Smoke Daddy next door
Music	Garage alternative
Bar Type	Dive Bar, Music Venue

Not much has changed at Phyllis' since accordionist Phyllis Jaskot opened the bar in 1954. Jaskot bought Harriet's Inn and transformed the place into a polka club, making it Wicker Park's oldest live music venue. Jaskot ran Phyllis' Musical Inn during the heyday of Polish Broadway (this section of Division Street) when the infamous Chicago novelist Nelson Algren prowled the neighborhood and would stop by for a drink (he got around). The vintage black & white wallpaper depicting piano keys, top hats, and canes is found above the bar today. Back then, just about every other building on the strip was a tavern, with names like *Red Goose Inn* (now Smoke Daddy), *Midnight Inn* (now Mac's), and *Rite Liquors* (still there). Phyllis' is now owned by former bike messenger, Clem Jaskot, who continues the musical tradition of his family. While the polka bands of Phyllis' day have yielded to groups that typically play garage alternative, the Musical Inn also attracts jazz musicians on Mondays and slam poets on Tuesdays. Most bands playing at Phyllis' are unknown, though Veruca Salt played a gig there just prior to their breakout single, *Seether*, in 1994. Bonuses: graffiti-filled restrooms and a mysterious door in the west wall leading to a beer garden that fills an entire lot and features picnic tables, ping-pong, and basketball—yep, there's even a hoop out there.

NEARBY   Smoke Daddy – 1804 W. Division St.
Mac's – 1801 W. Division St.
Moonshine – 1824 W. Division St.

SIMILAR   **FORMER NELSON ALGREN HAUNTS**
Rainbo Club – 1150 N. Damen Ave.
Gold Star Bar – 1755 W. Division St.
Lottie's Pub – 1925 W. Cortland St.
INDIE MUSIC HAVENS
Mutiny – 2428 N. Western Ave. (punk, free)
Empty Bottle – 1035 N. Western Ave.
  (indie rock)
Hideout – 1354 W. Wabansia Ave. (indie folk)

TRIVIA   What famous Chicago pizza chain (est. 1966) is
known for encouraging graffiti from patrons?

NOTES   _____

_____

_____

_____

_____

_____

ANSWER: Gino's East.

POPS FOR CHAMPAGNE

601 N. State St. (600N, 0E)
Chicago, IL 60610
(312) 266-7677

Website	www.popsforchampagne.com
Neighborhood	River North
Open 'til & Cover	2am daily (closed Sun); $8–15 for jazz
Drinks	125 champagnes, 17 beers, 31 wines
Food	Small plates (hot & cold), lunch Fri/Sat
Music	Jazz trios, bigger acts on weekends
Bar Type	Jazz Club, Cocktail Lounge

Pops for Champagne has the largest selection of bubbly in the Midwest, and it has been so since the bar opened in March 1982. That was the year proprietor Tom Verhey hired Chicago architect John Nelson to convert a grocery store into a neighborhood bar that would serve 13 champagnes and a limited bar menu. The idea came to Verhey after visiting Reiss' Champagne Bar in Vienna while working for Bell & Howell. In August 1986, the adjacent property was acquired and transformed into a jazz club, and the original space was converted into Star Bar. Following Bastille Day 2006, Pops for Champagne closed for a short time and re-opened at its present location. The former space was remodeled into Kirkwood Bar & Grill by Four Corners Tavern Group. Once seated at Pops, you'll want to pour through the leather-bound menu of 125 champagnes, including non-vintage, vintage, grower-producer, prestige cuvées, rosés, and sparkling wines. Pricing ranges from $45 to $1,500 a bottle, with a dozen available by the glass. A separate small plates menu features caviar, oysters, cheese plates, flatbreads, and chocolate fondue. Jazz is performed downstairs at Pops for Jazz, with regular trios Tue–Thu ($8) and headliners on Fri/Sat ($15). Pops draws tourists and area residents that know how to impress the bejesus out of a date. Some rue the day that Pops moved from its cozy environs in Lakeview but, as they say, c'est la vie…

NEARBY   The Joynt – 650 N. Dearborn St.
Excalibur Nightclub – 632 N. Dearborn St.
Redhead Piano Bar – 16 W. Ontario St.

SIMILAR   **OTHER LIBATION SPECIALISTS**
Webster's Wine Bar – 1480 W. Webster Ave. (wine)
Duke of Perth – 2913 N. Clark St. (Scotch)
Delilah's – 2771 N. Lincoln Ave. (Bourbon)
ALL THAT JAZZ
Jazz Showcase – 806 S. Plymouth Ct.
BackRoom – 1007 N. Rush St.
Green Mill Cocktail Lounge –
  4802 N. Broadway

TRIVIA   Who is credited with saying that enjoying
champagne is like "drinking stars"?

NOTES   _____

_____

_____

_____

_____

_____

ANSWER: *Benedictine monk, Dom Perignon.*

PUMP ROOM

1301 N. State Pkwy. (1300N, 0E)
Chicago, IL 60610
(312) 266-0360

Website	www.pumproom.com
Neighborhood	Gold Coast
Open 'til & Cover	11pm (1am Fri/Sat); never a cover
Drinks	Champagne, sage margaritas
Food	Breakfast, lunch, multi-course dinner
Music	Live piano jazz every Fr/Sat at 8pm
Bar Type	Hotel Bar, Restaurant

Located in the Ambassador East Hotel, the Pump Room is the last hotel bar from the Railroad Age, a time when celebrities dropped by on layovers between the Super Chief and the Twentieth Century Limited. Hotelier Ernie Byfield opened the Pump Room in 1938, inspired by the eighteenth-century original still operating today in Bath, England, where patrons could drink natural mineral water pumped into an indoor fountain and where royalty first mixed with commoners. Byfield's Pump Room became a celebrity magnet when Broadway actress Gertrude Lawrence held court in Booth One for 90 days straight while performing in town. Since then, Booth One has hosted many from the A-List: Bogart & Bacall got bombed on their honeymoon, John Barrymore had his drinks watered down, Salvador Dali drew on a tablecloth, and Sonny Bono was the first allowed in without a jacket. Frank Sinatra famously sings, "Chicago is...the jumping Pump Room," in the song *Chicago*, though he favored the Green Booth as it could seat eight people. The Portfolio Hotel Group and executive chef Nick Sutton run the Pump Room today. You'll still find oak paneling, fine china, chandeliers of Waterford crystal, and a wall of celebrity photos. Long gone are the walls of deep blue felt, white leather booths with tableside phones, flaming swords, and coffee boys wearing white turbans—but the Pump Room's elegance and legacy remain.

NEARBY	3rd Coast Café & Wine Bar – 1260 N. Dearborn St.
	Zebra Lounge – 1220 N. State Pkwy.
	PJ Clarke's – 1204 N. State Pkwy.
SIMILAR	**CELEBRITY HANGOUTS**
	Miller's Pub – 134 S. Wabash Ave.
	Green Mill Cocktail Lounge – 4802 N. Broadway
	Kingston Mines – 2548 N. Halsted St.
	MODERN HOTEL BARS
	Whiskey Blue – 172 W. Adams St. (W Hotel)
	The Bar at the Peninsula – 108 E. Superior St.
	Lockwood – 17 E. Monroe St. (Palmer House)
TRIVIA	What singer was refused entry to the Pump Room for not wearing a jacket?

NOTES

_____

_____

_____

_____

_____

ANSWER: Phil Collins, who recorded No Jacket Required in response.

QUENCHERS SALOON

2401 N. Western Ave. (2400N, 2400W)
Chicago, IL 60647
(773) 276-9730

Website	www.quenchers.com
Neighborhood	Bucktown
Open 'til & Cover	2am (3am Sat); never a cover
Drinks	Over 250 beers, including 16 on tap
Food	Sandwiches, pizza, chili, tater tots
Music	Open mic, jazz, the Polkaholics
Bar Type	Neighborhood Tavern, Beer Bar

Before the microbrewery explosion, there was Quenchers, Chicago's original beer bar. The initial owners transformed what had been Jug-Full Liquors since 1946 into "an oasis for young urban professionals outside of the Loop and Lincoln Park" in 1979. That didn't draw the crowds, so Earle Johnson, formerly with Berghoff (p. 2), joined the Quenchers team with the idea of expanding the beer selection to eight on tap and 40 in bottles—inspired by local restaurants Ranalli's Pizza and Weinkeller in Berwyn, and unheard of for a bar. Johnson ultimately took ownership and Quenchers today offers almost 250 ales, especially enjoyed during the Annual European Beer Tour held for ten days beginning the day after Thanksgiving. There are a few options for the tour but your best bet is the $30 option that gets you seven beers of your choosing, a commemorative T-shirt, beer glass, cheese & sausage plate, and a Polaroid picture of you to attach to your European beer "passport." For additional fun, Quenchers sponsors the annual Walk to Wrigley, a three-mile pub crawl with eleven stops concluding with a Cubs game at the ballpark (arguably making it a twelve-bar crawl). For entertainment, Quenchers hosts music, comedy, and open mic seven nights a week. Quenchers also features a good selection of hard liquor, from single-malt Scotch and bourbon to cognac and tequila. The bar only takes cash but they do have an ATM.

NEARBY	Mutiny – 2428 N. Western Ave.
	Bob Inn – 2609 W. Fullerton Ave.
	The Corner – 2224 N. Leavitt St.
SIMILAR	**TOP BEER BARS**
	Hopleaf – 5148 N. Clark St.
	Map Room – 1949 N. Hoyne Ave.
	Goose Island Brew Pub – 1800 N. Clybourn Ave.
	ECLECTIC LIVE PERFORMANCES
	Weeds Tavern – 1555 N. Dayton St.
	Liar's Club – 1665 W. Fullerton Ave.
	Phyllis' Musical Inn – 1800 W. Division St.
TRIVIA	What is the only other Chicago bar to serve Pripp's from Sweden?

NOTES

_____

_____

_____

_____

_____

_____

_____

RAINBO CLUB

1800 W. Division St. (1200N, 1800W)
Chicago, IL 60622
(773) 486-9862

Website	None
Neighborhood	Ukrainian Village
Open 'til & Cover	2am (3am Sat); never a cover
Drinks	Pabst Blue Ribbon, cheap cocktails
Food	Only of the "food for thought" variety
Music	Indie music spun on an actual turntable
Bar Type	Dive Bar, Neighborhood Tavern

"Ukie Village" was a different place prior to the gentrification that ramped up dramatically in the 1990s. The neighborhood used to be poor, blue collar, and predominantly Polish. This was the attraction to Chicago novelist Nelson Algren, who reveled in Chicago's seedy underbelly and frequented Rainbo Club for its burlesque shows, once featured on its clamshell stage (still there today). The impoverished, crusty regulars that Algren so cherished are emulated by many of the nuevo-bohemians who now call the place home. Dating back to 1936, the Rainbo Club, some speculate, is one of the places Algren brought Simone de Beauvoir, with whom he had a torrid affair during her Chicago visit, even though she was the lifelong companion of Jean-Paul Sartre. Rainbo Club is also said to have inspired Algren's fictional tavern, the Tug & Maul, in his National Book Award winner, *The Man with the Golden Arm* (1949), later adapted into a movie of the same name starring Frank Sinatra (1955). Rainbo Club was also featured in *High Fidelity* with John Cusack (the proposal scene), and many believe that the cover to Chicago indie rocker Liz Phair's first album, *Exile in Guyville* (notable for her exposed nipple), was taken in the Rainbo Club's photo booth. Instead of windows, Rainbo Club offers a display case of local artwork behind panes of glass, which purportedly were installed during Prohibition to absorb noise from the jumpin' speakeasy inside.

NEARBY   Easy Bar – 1944 W. Division St.
InnJoy – 2051 W. Division St.
Small Bar – 2049 W. Division St.

SIMILAR   **NELSON ALGREN HAUNTS**
Phyllis' Musical Inn – 1800 W. Division St.
Gold Star Bar – 1755 W. Division St.
Lottie's Pub – 1925 W. Cortland St.
TODAY'S BOHEMIAN HANGS
Charleston – 2076 N. Hoyne Ave.
Skylark – 2149 S. Halsted St.
Hungry Brain – 2319 W. Belmont Ave.

TRIVIA   *The Man with the Golden Arm* was Hollywood's
first "drug movie" depicting what narcotic?

NOTES   _____

_____

_____

_____

_____

_____

_____

ANSWER: Heroin.

RESI'S BIERSTUBE

2034 W. Irving Park Rd. (4000N, 2100W)
Chicago, IL 60618
(773) 472-1749

Website	None
Neighborhood	North Center
Open 'til & Cover	2am (3am Sat); never a cover
Drinks	Beer: 40 total, weiss & more on tap
Food	Sausages, pork schnitzel
Music	German oompah & other oddities
Bar Type	German, Neighborhood Tavern

Resi's has the same feel today as when it opened in 1965 by a German carpenter named Horst, who named the bar after his wife Theresa (for which "Resi" is the Bavarian nickname). Herbert and Ingeborg Stober, an immigrant couple hailing from Karlsruhe, Germany, bought Resi's in 1971. Most of the décor today at Resi's comes from Herbert's personal collection. For instance, the wooden beer wagon behind the bar was given to Stober by the Pschorr Brewery in Munich for selling the most Weiss beer (German white ale) in America, of which he was the first to import. Love him or hate him—Stober was also the first to import Jägermeister to Chicago. The building housing Resi's has been a bar since at least 1913 when it served as a tied house for a local brewery and was reputed to be a speakeasy owned by a cohort of Al Capone during Prohibition. The plethora of phone lines found in the basement by subsequent ownership suggests it was a bookmaking operation as well. Not only is the rear patio one of the city's hidden gems with its lantern-lit tables and stately maple trees, but it's also the city's oldest beer garden. Many of Chicago's German bars originally featured beer gardens, but they were banned during World War II to prevent Germans from congregating outside. The ban lasted until Resi's opened their beer garden in 1965 and paved the way for all those we love today—and for that we can say, *Danke schön!*

NEARBY	Laschet's Inn – 2119 W. Irving Park Rd. (German)
	O'Donovan's – 2100 W. Irving Park Rd.
	Glunz Bavarian Haus – 4128 N. Lincoln (German)
SIMILAR	**GERMANIC RESTAURANTS & TAVERNS**
	Chicago Brauhaus – 4732 N. Lincoln Ave.
	Mirabell – 3454 W. Addison St. (Austrian)
	17 West at the Berghoff – 17 W. Adams St.
	OLDEST CHICAGO BEER GARDENS
	Moody's Pub – 5910 N. Broadway
	Happy Village – 1059 N. Wolcott Ave.
	Weeds Tavern – 1555 N. Dayton St.
TRIVIA	What does the sign above the bar reading *Man hat kein Schlitz, denn hat kein bier* mean?
NOTES	_____
	_____
	_____
	_____
	_____
	_____

ANSWER: *If one has no Schlitz, then one has no beer.*

RIVER SHANNON

425 W. Armitage Ave. (2000N, 400W)
Chicago, IL 60614
(312) 944-5087

Website	www.rushanddivision.com
Neighborhood	Lincoln Park
Open 'til & Cover	2am (3am Sat); never a cover
Drinks	Of the standard variety, plus Guinness
Food	Free peanuts
Music	Well-stocked jukebox
Bar Type	Meat Market, Irish Pub

Named for the waterway that runs from Carrick to Limerick back on the Emerald Isle, River Shannon has been an anchor for the evolving Lincoln Park bar scene for over 60 years. The pub opened in 1946 by the Cloherty Family and appealed to local firemen in a time that predated all of today's sports bars, swanky lounges, and meat markets that pepper the neighborhood. At the base of a stately, three-story brick building, River Shannon beckons with old-fashioned street lights, a tasteful green awning from which evergreens hang, a red-painted wooden façade, etched glass doors, and large picture windows that look out onto Armitage. Step inside and you'll find a smallish, one-room saloon with a long wooden Brunswick bar with a brass foot railing on your left and a smattering of cocktail tables on your right. The floor is covered in quarter-inch ceramic tiles with "RS" emblazoned upon them and the walls are paneled in mahogany wood and adorned with black & white photographs of baseball players like Babe Ruth pitching for the Red Sox. Sykes Williams once dazzled the crowd here in the 1970s with his piano playing. The overall feel of the River Shannon today is that of a polished Butch McGuire's (p. 24) or Lodge Tavern (p. 112), the latter of which is operated by the Lodge Management Group that owns River Shannon and several other Chicago tavern classics, mostly located a bit further south in the Gold Coast.

NEARBY   Stanley's Kitchen & Tap – 1970 N. Lincoln Ave.
Sedgwick's – 1935 N. Sedgwick St.
Gamekeepers Tavern & Grill –
1971 N. Lincoln Ave.

SIMILAR   **THROWBACK LINCOLN PARK SINGLES BARS**
Kincade's – 950 W. Armitage Ave.
Glascott's Groggery – 2158 N. Halsted St.
Burwood Tap – 724 W. Wrightwood Ave.
IRISH-TINGED NEIGHBORHOOD CLASSICS
Kelly's Pub – 949 W. Webster Ave.
Abbey Pub – 3420 N. Grace St.
Celtic Crossings – 751 N. Clark St.

TRIVIA   What annual Chicago pub crawl features River
Shannon as one of its first stops?

NOTES   _____

_____

_____

_____

_____

_____

ANSWER: *The dangerous "12 Bars of Christmas."*

ROSA'S LOUNGE

3420 W. Armitage Ave. (2000N, 3400W)
Chicago, IL 60647
(773) 342-0452

Website	www.rosaslounge.com
Neighborhood	Logan Square
Open 'til & Cover	2am (3am Sat); $5–15 cover
Drinks	Bottled domestic beer and cocktails
Food	Occasional cooking from Mama
Music	Full spectrum of blues
Bar Type	Blues Club

Rosa's Lounge opened in 1984, a dream fulfilled by Tony Mangiullo, once an aspiring blues drummer who met Junior Wells backstage at a jazz concert in his home country of Italy in 1978. Wells invited Mangiullo to Chicago, giving him his home address as well as that of the legendary former blues club Theresa's Lounge (p. 223). This prospect appealed to him more than running the fruit stand he inherited from his father, so he flew to Chicago. Mangiullo's mother followed her son shortly afterwards, intending to bring Tony back to run the family business. Instead, she was persuaded to stay and open a blues club with him. Rosa's Lounge was born. Since then, many Chicago blues legends who Tony first got to know on the South Side have spent time on Rosa's stage, including Billy Branch (on opening night), Junior Wells, Pinetop Perkins, Melvin Taylor, and even the Rolling Stones. Today, Mama Rosa can still be found tending bar and shooting some stick, while Tony works the room and occasionally sits in with the band. A wide range of blues is presented five nights a week to a crowd composed more of true blues enthusiasts than the usual conventioneers, tourists, and suburbanites that flock to Blues Alley in Lincoln Park. Other clubs may be more popular, but for those that have come to know it, Rosa's may be Chicago's most beloved blues joint—a place simply described as "real."

NEARBY	Whirlaway – 3224 W. Fullerton Ave.
	Bob Inn – 2609 W. Fullerton Ave.
	Mutiny – 2428 N. Western Ave.
SIMILAR	**BLUES CLUBS**
	B.L.U.E.S. – 2519 N. Halsted St.
	New Checkerboard Lounge – 5201 S. Harper Ct.
	Lee's Unleaded Blues –
	7401 S. South Chicago Ave.
	FAMILY-OWNED INSTITUTIONS
	Billy Goat Tavern – 430 N. Michigan Ave.
	17 West at the Berghoff – 17 W. Adams St.
	Jazz Showcase – 806 S. Plymouth Ct.
TRIVIA	What famous bluesman became Rosa's second husband in Chicago?
NOTES	_____
	_____
	_____
	_____
	_____
	_____

ANSWER: "Homesick" James Williamson.

SCHALLER'S PUMP

3714 S. Halsted St. (3700S, 800W)
Chicago, IL 60609
(773) 376-6332

Website	None
Neighborhood	Bridgeport
Open 'til & Cover	2am (3am Sat); never a cover
Drinks	Mostly domestics
Food	Butt steak: far better than it sounds
Music	Radio, live accordion on Fri/Sat
Bar Type	Neighborhood Tavern, Sports Bar

Schaller's Pump is the oldest, continuously running tavern in Chicago. Opened in 1881, the saloon operated under a different name until George "Harvey" Schaller purchased it at the end of Prohibition. Just ask today's third and fourth generation of Schallers to show you the concealed peephole from its speakeasy days (Hint: it's in the south wall). Above the bar, you'll find bullwhips from the Union Stock Yards, Carl Sandburg's inspiration for *Hog Butcher for the World*. Schaller's Pump refers to the mechanism that once pumped beer directly to the bar from the Ambrosia Brewery next door, where the parking lot now is. Schaller's today represents two American traditions: baseball and politics. Only a few blocks from the old and new Comiskey Parks (present corporate name withheld), Schaller's is a haven for White Sox fans and their respective clans. The district's Democratic headquarters is located across the street and Schaller's has served as a second office for no less than five of Chicago's Democratic mayors, all hailing from Bridgeport, including present and past Mayors Richard Daley. At the end of the day, Schaller's Pump is a classic Chicago tavern perfect for before and after Sox games and on St. Patty's Day. Be sure to have a shot to thank each of your dead relatives that cast their ballot in the most recent Democratic victory.

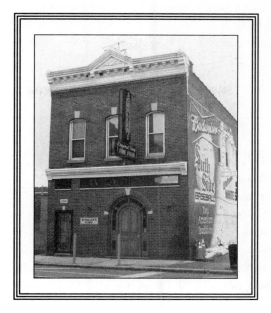

NEARBY	Bullpen Sports Bar – White Sox Park (right field)
	Shinnick's Pub – 3758 S. Union Ave. (since 1938)
	Mitchell's Tap – 3356 S. Halsted St. (was Puffer's)
SIMILAR	**CLASSIC NEIGHBORHOOD TAVERNS**
	Sterch's – 2238 N. Lincoln Ave.
	Charleston – 2076 N. Hoyne Ave.
	Guthries Tavern – 1300 W. Addison St.
	OLD-SCHOOL SPORTS BAR (NORTH SIDE)
	Slugger's – 3540 N. Clark St.
	Murphy's Bleachers – 3655 N. Sheffield Ave.
	Yak-zies on Clark – 3710 N. Clark St.
TRIVIA	Other than the Daleys, can you name the other three Democratic Bridgeport mayors?

NOTES

_____

_____

_____

_____

_____

_____

_____

ANSWER: Edward Kelly, Martin Kennelly, and Michael Bilandic.

SCHUBAS TAVERN

3159 N. Southport Ave. (3200N, 1400W)
Chicago, IL 60657
(773) 525-2508

Website	www.schubas.com
Neighborhood	Lakeview
Open 'til & Cover	2am (3am Sat); $5–25 cover (in rear)
Drinks	13 beers and Jägermeister on tap
Food	Served from Harmony Grill next door
Music	Regional & national rock and folk
Bar Type	Neighborhood Tavern, Music Venue

The Schlitz Brewery erected the building that now houses Schubas Tavern in 1903. At the time, Schlitz was the king of beers and had built 57 bars in Chicago. These "tied houses" were later sold off due to eventual legislation that forbade breweries from owning bars—not much gratitude considering that Joseph Schlitz donated thousands of gallons of beer and water to Chicago after the Great Fire of 1871. Schubas Tavern is one of only ten such masterpieces that remain and, thanks to the 1988 renovation by the current owners, is in superb condition. Chris and Mike Schuba opened Schubas in 1989, replacing the live music bar Gaspar's, previously the Bavarian Inn and a Mexican tavern before that. Chris once part-owned the now-defunct Everleigh Club (currently Tonic Room), named after a well-known Levee District bordello of the early 1900s. Schubas' exterior is adorned with herringbone-patterned brickwork and topped off by bas-relief Schlitz globes, the image found on Schlitz bottles. Schubas still sells the brew in brown bottles, a 1921 Schlitz product innovation to prevent sunlight from spoiling the beer before serving. Besides being a classic neighborhood bar, Schubas is also one of Chicago's premier rock and folk venues with top-notch sound and acoustics. Feeling peckish? Fairly decent pub grub is available from the adjacent Harmony Grill, opened in 1997 and under the same ownership.

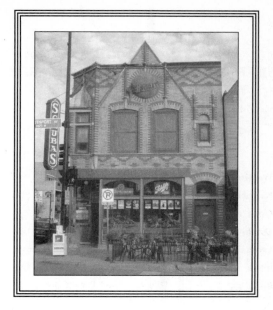

NEARBY	Schoolyard Tavern – 3258 N. Southport Ave.
	Joey's Brickhouse – 1258 W. Belmont Ave.
	Lincoln Tap Room – 3010 N. Lincoln Ave.
SIMILAR	**FORMER SCHLITZ BARS**
	Southport Lanes & Billiards –
	3325 N. Southport Ave.
	Floyd's Pub – 1944 N. Oakley Ave.
	Mac's American Pub – 1801 W. Division St.
	LOCAL FOLK MUSIC VENUES
	Abbey Pub – 3420 W. Grace St.
	Martyrs' – 3855 N. Lincoln Ave.
	Hideout – 1354 W. Wabansia Ave.
TRIVIA	What South African–led band appeared at Schubas in their early days?
NOTES	_____
	_____
	_____
	_____
	_____
	_____

SHEFFIELD'S WINE & BEER GARDEN

3258 N. Sheffield Ave. (3300N, 1000W)
Chicago, IL 60657
(773) 281-4989

Website	www.sheffieldschicago.com
Neighborhood	Lakeview
Open 'til & Cover	2am (3am Sat); never a cover
Drinks	24 beers on tap and 100 in bottles
Food	Back room barbeque, mmm-hmm
Music	No jukebox or live; bartender-spun
Bar Type	Neighborhood Tavern, Beer Bar

Sheffield's opened in 1980 and was originally conceived as both a tavern and a coffee house with theater performance space, the latter of which was known as the School Street Café. Since then, the tavern half won out and Sheffield's now features over 100 microbrews and Belgian beers, and six wines by the glass. On that first warm day of the year in Chicago that occurs sometime between March and July, nothing beats the beer garden at Sheffield's. It's routinely voted #1 in the city, largely due to its shady cottonwood trees, cascading vines along the brick walls, and the highly sought after picnic tables. In 2007, Sheffield's installed a kitchen serving both Memphis (sweet) and Texas (spicy) style baby back ribs, as well as "Half a Smoked Chicken" and BBQ brisket. Harkening back to its early days, the back room at Sheffield's hosts Reading Under the Influence (RUI), a reading series, "developed by a group of Chicago writers who happen to like drinking." RUI is held on the first Wednesday of every month, and features local writers and their works. Thursday nights is open mic comedy at 9pm. When asked, "If you could only go to one bar for the rest of your life, which would it be?" My answer is Sheffield's. It is true that the beer garden gets very crowded and, even on colder days in prime time, a line to get in stretches down the block. In either case, you just need to get here earlier.

NEARBY   Redmond's – 3358 N. Sheffield Ave.
Trader Todd's – 3216 N. Sheffield Ave.
Matilda – 3101 N. Sheffield Ave.

SIMILAR   **TOP LAKEVIEW PUBS**
Duke of Perth – 2913 N. Clark St.
Southport Lanes & Billiards –
    3325 N. Southport Ave.
Cullen's Bar & Grill – 3741 N. Southport Ave.
HUGE BEER SELECTION
Quenchers – 2401 N. Western Ave.
Hopleaf Bar – 5148 N. Clark St.
Map Room – 1949 N. Hoyne Ave.

TRIVIA   Who was Joseph Sheffield, namesake of this pub?

NOTES   _____

_____

_____

_____

_____

_____

ANSWER: *A train mogul, responsible for the Chicago and Rock Island Railroad.*

SHINNICK'S PUB

3758 S. Union Ave. (3800S, 700W)
Chicago, IL 60609
(773) 523-8591

Website	www.shinnicks.com
Neighborhood	Bridgeport
Open 'til & Cover	2am (3am Sat); never a cover
Drinks	Cheap domestic beer in cans
Food	Hot dogs in Bev's garage across the st.
Music	Jukebox, South Side–style
Bar Type	Neighborhood Tavern, Irish Pub

Shinnick's is as ignored by North Siders and bar guides as it is loved by the Bridgeport neighborhood surrounding it—and no one down here minds at all. While nearby Schaller's Pump (p. 166) is older and better known, the Shinnick's legacy begins circa 1890, when the pub was constructed with the original tin ceiling and mahogany Brunswick bar still in use today, possibly for the 1893 World's Columbian Exposition. The pub was first owned by the Shallow family and passed through a few hands (and Prohibition) until 1938 when it reached George W. Shinnick, Sr., and his wife Mary. The pub has been family-owned ever since. George Shinnick, Jr., took over with his wife Celine in 1966. Shinnick's Pub then battled through the next 30 years of urban decay and racial strife in Chicago, thanks to the nine Shinnick children who helped take care of the joint. The torch was passed in 1992 to the third generation of Shinnicks, and you'll encounter them behind the bar today. Non-Shinnicks actually do work for the pub and, in fact, their website honors all 85 former bartenders, 16 thoughtfully listed with angel wings. You can hoist a can of beer in their honor, just as the regulars do, as did their fathers and grandfathers before them. Given its proximity to Comiskey Park, you can also expect a rowdy time after Sox wins. Bar Olympians will also find Golden Tee, darts, and cornhole outside in summer.

NEARBY   Cobblestones Bar & Grill – 514 W. Pershing Rd.
Schaller's Pump – 3714 S. Halsted St.
Bernice and John's – 3238 S. Halsted St.

SIMILAR   **NON-BRIDGEPORT SOX BARS**
Cork & Kerry – 10614 S. Western Ave.
Kroll's South Loop – 1736 S. Michigan Ave.
Bob Inn – 2609 W. Fullerton Ave.
NORTH SIDE TRADITION
Cubby Bear – 1059 W. Addison St.
Murphy's Bleachers – 3655 N. Sheffield Ave.
Yak-zies on Clark – 3710 N. Clark St.

TRIVIA   What does the surname *Sionnagh* (anglicized to *Shinnick*) mean in Gaelic?

NOTES   _____

_____

_____

_____

_____

_____

_____

ANSWER: *Fox.*

SIGNATURE LOUNGE

875 N. Michigan Ave. (John Hancock Building)
96th Fl. (900N, 100E)
Chicago, IL 60611
(312) 787-9596

Website	www.signatureroom.com
Neighborhood	Magnificent Mile
Open 'til & Cover	12:30am (1:30am Fri/Sat); no cover
Drinks	24 signature martinis, champagne
Food	Limited appetizers, sangers, desserts
Music	Live jazz 8pm–midnight, Sun–Thu
Bar Type	Cocktail Lounge, Tourist Trap

The Signature Lounge is one of the highest bars in the world, located on the 96th floor of the John Hancock Building and one story above the posh Signature Room restaurant. Both offer stunning views of downtown and Lake Michigan, and visibility up to 60 miles that spans four states on a clear day. The Signature Lounge opened in 1993 by former staffers Rick Roman and Nick Pyknis, replacing the corporate-owned Images. The space originally opened as Sybaris Lounge in 1970, a year after Skidmore, Owings & Merrill constructed their 100-story masterpiece. The building entrance on Chestnut leads you to a high-speed elevator that takes 40 seconds to ascend 1,000 feet—or 25 feet per second! No wonder your ears pop. While the restaurant is formal, there is no dress code for what locals lewdly call, "The Top of the 'Cock." All are welcome, be they tourists in T-shirts or wedding receptions. Cocktails run about $13, but they're still cheaper than tickets to the observatory ($15 per adult) two floors below. The lounge also serves a nice selection of champagne, cognacs, single malt scotch, and armagnacs. Your best bet: Bypass the rope line for views of the Loop, and grab a stool across from the island bar to enjoy your beverage while gazing at "The Grid," just as you would flying into O'Hare. The ladies' room has a smashing view of the Loop, while the men's has nothing.

NEARBY	Coq d'Or – 140 E. Walton St. (Drake Hotel)
	The Martini Bar – 163 E. Walton Pl. (Knickerbocker)
	Seasons Bar – 120 E. Delaware Pl. (Four Seasons)
SIMILAR	**OTHER STUNNING VIEWS**
	Roof – 201 N. State St. (Wit Hotel, 27th Fl.)
	C-View – 166 E. Superior St. (Affinia Hotel, 26th Fl.)
	Vertigo Sky Bar – 2 W. Erie St. (Dana Hotel, 26th Fl.)
	NEARBY GOLD COAST LOUNGES
	Le Passage – 937 N. Rush St.
	Luxbar – 18 E. Bellevue Pl.
	The Bar at the Peninsula Hotel – 108 E. Superior St.
TRIVIA	The lounge's name is a play on words, can you figure it out?
NOTES	_____
	_____
	_____
	_____

ANSWER: *The signature of John Hancock.*

SIMON'S TAVERN

5210 N. Clark St. (5200N, 1600W)
Chicago, IL 60640
(773) 878-0894

Website	www.simonstavern.com
Neighborhood	Andersonville
Open 'til & Cover	2am (3am Sat); never a cover
Drinks	Pripp's, Schlitz, glögg (winter)
Food	A ginger cookie with your glögg
Music	Indy jukebox, small bands on weekends
Bar Type	Neighborhood Tavern, Dive Bar

Original owner Simon Lundberg emigrated from Sweden in the early 1900s and became a citizen by fighting for the U.S. in WWI. After the war, he opened a grocery store in Chicago's Swedish neighborhood, Andersonville, and sold whiskey with coffee during Prohibition. This practice was so profitable that he bought a bigger place at the current address and ran a speakeasy out of the basement called the No Name Club. Lundberg transformed the grocery into Simon's Tavern in 1934 following Prohibition in an Art Deco style that evoked being on the *S.S. Normandie*, the largest ocean liner of the time. Simon's cashed paychecks, as many distrusted banks after the stock market crash of 1929, and charged nothing for this service because most of the cash doled out ($14,000 per week) was paid back to wash down sandwiches from the free payday buffet. The cashier's room under the stairs, with its 3" thick steel door and bulletproof glass are all still there today. Lundberg's son Roy took over following his death, but he's immortalized in the portrait next to *The Deer Hunter's Ball* mural. You'll drink for free if you can name the five animals hidden in the mural, located somewhere beneath 80 years of nicotine buildup. Roy passed the place on to Scott Martin in 1994, a local entrepreneur with Swedish roots. Simon's today is the last Swedish tavern in the neighborhood and serves as a bridge between old Swedish Andersonville and the hipper potpourri of folks that have since moved in. *Skål!*

NEARBY	Hopleaf Bar – 5148 N. Clark St.
	Farragut's – 5240 N. Clark St.
	Charlie's Ale House – 5308 N. Clark St.
SIMILAR	**ETHNIC CHICAGO LEGENDS**
	Chicago Brauhaus – 4732 N. Lincoln Ave. (German)
	Nisei Lounge – 3439 N. Sheffield Ave. (Japanese)
	Happy Village – 1059 N. Wolcott Ave. (Polish)
	NAUTICAL THEME
	Twin Anchors – 1655 N. Sedgwick St.
	Castaways – 1603 N. Lakeshore Dr.
	Cove Lounge – 1750 E. 55th St.
TRIVIA	Why the fish-holding-a-cocktail logo of Simon's?
NOTES	_____
	_____
	_____
	_____
	_____
	_____

ANSWER: _It's a "pickled" herring, a Swedish dish._

SLUGGERS

3540 N. Clark St. (3600N, 1000W)
Chicago, IL 60657
(773) 248-0055

Website	www.sluggerschicago.com
Neighborhood	Wrigleyville
Open 'til & Cover	2am (3am Sat); $3–5 cover for music
Drinks	15 taps, Old Style tall boys, Jello shots
Food	Wings, burgers, pizza until midnight
Music	Dueling pianos Fri/Sat & home games
Bar Type	Sports Bar, Piano Lounge

This self-proclaimed "world class sports bar" is sure to entertain anyone, at least for a night—if not for the amusements, then definitely for the lively crowd. The Strauss Family opened Sluggers in 1985, and only Cubby Bear (p. 44) and Murphy's Bleachers (p. 132) are older in Wrigleyville. The main floor at Sluggers features a large island bar, 40 TVs, an impressive display of Cubs and other Chicago sports memorabilia, and a stage for dancing when DJs play on weekends. The back room features seven pool tables. Think you can hit a 90 mph fastball? Head to the batting cages in the Upper Deck, above the main bar. Don't worry: pitch speeds drop down to 60 mph for baseball. They also offer slow-pitch softball cages, air hockey, Pop-a-Shot, skee-ball, and hi-ball—the latter of which is like playing basketball on a trampoline (only available in the off-season). If that's not enough, another room hosts dueling pianos every weekend and after Cubs home games à la Howl at the Moon. Patrons are encouraged to get up and dance on the pianos by jumping on a brass pole between them. Sluggers used to host dwarf wrestling by the "Half Pint Brawlers" but abandoned it in 2002 due to complaints. As you might guess, Sluggers attracts suburbanites and out-of-towners, while city dwellers tend to have a love-hate relationship with the place. If you want to see Sluggers in its full glory, be sure to visit after a Friday or Saturday afternoon Cubs game.

NEARBY	Wild Hare – 3530 N. Clark St. (reggae)
	Goose Island Wrigleyville – 3535 N. Clark St.
	John Barleycorn Wrigleyville – 3524 N. Clark St.
SIMILAR	**SPORTS ENTERTAINMENT EMPORIUMS**
	ESPN Zone – 43 E. Ohio St.
	Dave & Buster's – 1030 N. Clark St.
	Joe's Sports Bar – 940 W. Weed St.
	PIANO CROWD PARTICIPATION
	Howl at the Moon – 26 W. Hubbard St.
	Redhead Piano Bar – 16 W. Ontario St.
	Zebra Lounge – 1220 N. State Pkwy.
TRIVIA	Behind the dueling pianos is a mural depicting Cubs #14. Who wore this number?

NOTES

_____

_____

_____

_____

_____

_____

_____

ANSWER: *"Let's Play Two" Ernie Banks.*

SOUTHPORT LANES & BILLIARDS

3325 N. Southport Ave. (3300N, 1400W)
Chicago, IL 60657
(773) 472-1601

Website	www.southportlanes.com
Neighborhood	Lakeview
Open 'til & Cover	2am (3am Sat); never a cover
Drinks	Over 40 beers, 22 single-malt Scotches
Food	Tasty and cleverly named pub grub
Music	Unremarkable jukebox
Bar Type	Neighborhood Tavern, Bowling Alley

Southport Lanes was built in 1922 and operated as a Schlitz Brewery tied house, meaning that only Schlitz beer could be served there. Note the enormous Schlitz globe logo in bas-relief on the building's north side, similar to that of nearby Schubas (p. 168). Not only did the tavern operate as a speakeasy during Prohibition, but it also featured a brothel upstairs, just like the Cabaret Room at Subterranean (2011 W. North), both of which reformer Billy Sunday couldn't shut down. Prostitution was (and still is) illegal in Chicago, so the owner had to subtly advertise the delights found upstairs. He did this by having M.K. Siegner paint murals depicting nymphs frolicking in negligees, still seen today above the bar and bowling alley. Southport Lanes was purchased in 1991 by Spare Time Events, which also runs Seven Ten and Riverview Tavern. Fortunately, the new owners did not mess with what made the original, Leo's Southport Lanes owned by Leo and Ella Beitz, a much-loved neighborhood tavern. Bowling on four maple lanes is primarily available to private parties, reserved in advance. Pins are set manually by pinboys: "If you see legs, don't bowl!" Tips are placed into a ball and rolled down the gutter afterwards. Southport Lanes also features billiards on several regulation-sized tables and the sidewalk patio offers prime seating in warmer times. Southport Lanes is also home to one of the best pub bathrooms in the city, upstairs. Who knew?

NEARBY	Schoolyard Tavern – 3258 N. Southport Ave.
	Justin's – 3358 N. Southport Ave.
	Mystic Celt – 3443 N. Southport Ave.
SIMILAR	**BOWLING TAVERNS**
	Seven Ten – 2747 N. Lincoln Ave.
	10pin Bowling Lounge – 330 N. State St.
	Fireside Bowl – 2648 W. Fullerton Ave.
	FORMER SCHLITZ TAVERNS
	Schubas Tavern – 3159 N. Southport Ave.
	Floyd's Pub – 1944 N. Oakley Ave.
	Mac's American Pub – 1801 W. Division St.
TRIVIA	What politically incorrect adornment can be found at Southport Lanes?

NOTES

_____

_____

_____

_____

_____

_____

_____

ANSWER: A wooden "Native American."

STERCH'S

2238 N. Lincoln Ave. (2200N, 600W)
Chicago, IL 60614
(773) 281-2653

Website	www.sterchs.com
Neighborhood	Lincoln Park
Open 'til & Cover	2am (3am Sat); never a cover
Drinks	6 beers on tap; Templeton Rye
Food	Bags of YoHo potato chips
Music	Jukebox with classic rock and jazz
Bar Type	Neighborhood Tavern, Dive Bar

A plaque on the southern wall reads, "House of Sterch, Nov. 18, 1971," referring to the day Sterch's opened, replacing a bar called the Volstead Act (for the law that created Prohibition). Sterch's is a mashing of the names of the original owners Harlan Stern and Bob Smerch. The duo initially made their mark serving "french-fried carrots" for 25¢ in white bunny suits during the Body Politic street festival organized by community theater groups in the late '60s and early '70s. Back then, this stretch of Lincoln Avenue was part of the counter-culture scene, and Abbie Hoffman and the Chicago Seven are said to have frequented Sterch's after their conviction was overturned for inciting the riots during the 1968 Democratic National Convention. Other former regulars include movie critic Roger Ebert, director and talk show host Bonnie Hunt, Betty Thomas of *Hill Street Blues*, and William Peterson of *CSI*. Hunter S. Thompson once smashed up a urinal and later sent a check to cover the damage, with an additional $2,500 tacked on to account for potential future visits. Local folksinger Fred Holstein, a fixture at Sterch's up to his death, added the bar sign from his self-named former bar to those on the walls from other taverns that also have gone to the Last Call in the Sky, including O'Rourke's, Orphans, and Bill & Mary's (owned by Smerch's parents). Today, Sterch's is an actual pub surrounded by those that merely claim to be.

NEARBY   Lion Head Pub – 2251 N. Lincoln Ave.
Kendall's – 2263 N. Lincoln Ave.
Wise Fools Pub – 2270 N. Lincoln Ave.

SIMILAR   **SOUL OF THE NEIGHBORHOOD**
Schaller's Pump – 3714 S. Halsted St.
Simon's Tavern – 5210 N. Clark St.
Cunneen's – 1424 W. Devon Ave.
FORMER COUNTER-CULTURE PUBS
Old Town Ale House – 219 W. North Ave.
Four Farthings – 2060 N. Cleveland Ave.
Heartland Café – 7000 N. Glenwood Ave.

TRIVIA   What former White Sox owner watched opening day at Sterch's the year after he sold the team?

NOTES   _____
_____
_____
_____
_____
_____
_____

ANSWER: *Bill Veeck (1982).*

TUFANO'S VERNON PARK TAP

1073 W. Vernon Park Pl. (1100W, 700S)
Chicago, IL 60607
(312) 733-3393

Website	None
Neighborhood	Tri-Taylor
Open 'til & Cover	10pm Tu–Th, 11pm w/e, 9pm Sun; n/c
Drinks	No tap beer, 16 wines under $20
Food	Inexpensive Southern Italian
Music	Only silverware on porcelain
Bar Type	Italian Joint, Neighborhood Tavern

Taylor Street is known for its Old World Italian restaurants but Tufano's Vernon Park Tap is one of the only neighborhood taverns around (if you can find it). Opened first as a bakery in 1930, the Vernon Park Tap has been run over the decades entirely by the Tufano Family. It's now in the hands of Joey DiBuono, grandson of the original owners. Tufano's has no sign and is nestled into the residential side street from which it takes its name (best accessible via Racine Avenue because of the ever-growing UIC campus). Just inside is a bar where locals gather to watch the TV, above a photo of heavyweight champion, Rocky Marciano, and other famous Italians who have visited Tufano's, like Frank Sinatra, Tommy Lasorda, Dan Marino, and local politicians—all of whom appreciated a dining experience free from bother. Even Chicago novelist Nelson Algren came in before Sox games in the 1960s. Algren appreciated the neighborhood feel that still exists today. The casual, no-frills dining room is dominated by a large chalkboard illustrating the menu (there are none of the printed variety), highlighted by chicken piccata, eggplant parmesan, lemon chicken, and fried calamari. The waitstaff are all relatives or family friends, and service is no-nonsense. Payment is cash only, reservations are taken only for groups of eight or more, and the joint gets busy on weekends and before Bulls and Blackhawks games at nearby United Center. Zoned street parking makes $5 valet parking a better deal than a $60 ticket from Chicago's finest.

NEARBY	Hawkeye's Bar & Grill – 1458 W. Taylor St.
	Drum & Monkey – 1435 W. Taylor St.
	Jay's on Taylor – 1421 W. Taylor St.
SIMILAR	**NEIGHBORHOOD ITALIAN**
	Club Lago – 331 W. Superior St. (River North)
	Club Lucky – 1824 W. Wabansia (Wicker Park)
	Italian Village – 71 W. Monroe St. (Loop)
	BEST OF TAYLOR STREET
	Rosebud – 1500 W. Taylor St.
	Francesca's – 1400 W. Taylor St.
	Tuscany – 1014 W. Taylor St.
TRIVIA	What public housing project was built in the middle of Little Italy and is now largely demolished?
NOTES	_____
	_____
	_____
	_____
	_____
	_____

ANSWER: *Jane Addams Homes.*

TWIN ANCHORS

1655 N. Sedgwick St. (1700N, 400W)
Chicago, IL 60614
(312) 266-1616

Website	www.twinanchorsribs.com
Neighborhood	Old Town Triangle
Open 'til & Cover	2am (3am Sat); never a cover
Drinks	Cocktails and domestic brews
Food	Ribs, steaks, and not much else
Music	Rat Pack, pre-1980 jukebox
Bar Type	Neighborhood Tavern, Rib Joint

Twin Anchors stands out as the most historic rib joint in Chicago. The building dates back to 1881 and the first floor operated as a saloon as early as 1890 up until Prohibition, when the place was a speakeasy operated by Don and Ethel Humphrey called Tante Lee Soft Drinks. Bob Walters and Herb Eldean opened the Twin Anchors we all know and love in 1932. Both were members of the Chicago Yacht Club, and Eldean was the master of Monroe Harbor, hence the pair of wooden anchors in the back and the rest of the nautical theme. Even without a kitchen at first, Bob's wife became so well known for cooking ribs on Sunday nights for the regulars that a kitchen was later built to accommodate increasing demand. The Tuzi family took ownership of Twin Anchors in 1978, remodeled it in 1990, and continues to operate the place today in its original spirit. Even Frank Sinatra came in for baby back ribs in the '60s, and preferred the booth to the immediate right of the side door that now leads out to the sidewalk café. Many local celebrities love "The Twin" these days, including director and talk show host Bonnie Hunt who filmed *Return to Me* (2000) almost entirely on the premises. A scene from *The Dark Knight* was also filmed here. Just remember: "Positively No Dancing," particularly for any that fall prey to the Electric Slide, as this once interfered with waitresses carrying plates of ribs back in the disco era, leading to the ban.

NEARBY	Marge's Still – 1758 N. Sedgwick St.
	Bricks – 1909 N. Lincoln Ave.
	Sedgwick's – 1935 N. Sedgwick St.
SIMILAR	**OLD TOWN CLASSICS**
	Old Town Ale House – 219 W. North Ave.
	Fireplace Inn – 1448 N. Wells St.
	Burton Place – 1447 N. Wells St. (for late-night)
	RIB JOINTS
	Smoke Daddy – 1804 W. Division St.
	Miller's Pub – 134 S. Wabash Ave.
	Chicago Joe's – 2256 W. Irving Park Rd.
TRIVIA	Twin Anchors is what former Cub Hall-of-Famer's favorite place for ribs?

NOTES

_____

_____

_____

_____

_____

_____

_____

ANSWER: *Ryne Sandberg.*

WEBSTER'S WINE BAR

1480 W. Webster Ave. (2200N, 1500W)
Chicago, IL 60614
(773) 868-0608

Website	www.websterwinebar.com
Neighborhood	Lincoln Park
Open 'til & Cover	2am (3am Sat); never a cover
Drinks	500 bottles of wine, 30 "on tap" (glass)
Food	Small plates, cheese, pizza, seafood
Music	Soulful Sticky Lupree, free on Monday
Bar Type	Wine Bar, Haunted

Webster's is Chicago's oldest wine bar, opened in the fall of 1994 by the husband-and-wife team Tom MacDonald and Janan Asfour. The self-described "burned-out litigation consultants looking for a lifestyle change" replaced the Robert Henry Adams Fine Art gallery. Webster's is located across from Webster Place cinema, making it the perfect location for pre- and post-film drinks. An impressive variety of wine is offered in this intimate, candlelit space. Wines can be enjoyed by the glass and poured from taps behind the bar, and are available in flights and bottles (most around $40), and during monthly tastings—appropriate for occasional swiller and oenophile alike. A leather-bound menu illustrates the small plate and dessert offerings. They do carry a few beers in bottles, but why are you drinking beer here anyway? The main room is fairly small and crowded on weekends, and additional seating upstairs handles overflow. The second floor of this century-old building served as a brothel many years ago. A lounge up there also sports a fireplace, hosts the 2nd Story storytelling group every month ($10), and may be haunted. A male apparition has been seen, and the staff has heard disembodied footsteps. Bonuses: Free parking behind the movie theater and a pleasant sidewalk café in summer. Many other wine bars have since come and gone, but it is Webster's Wine Bar that has legs. Go for a glass and leave after a few bottles...

NEARBY   Green Dolphin Street – 2200 N. Ashland Ave.
Flounder's – 2201 N. Clybourn Ave.
Charlie's on Webster – 1224 W. Webster Ave.

SIMILAR   **NEIGHBORHOOD WINE BARS**
Joie de Vin – 1744 W. Balmoral Ave.
  (Andersonville)
Enoteca Roma – 2144 W. Division St.
  (Wicker Park)
DOC Wine Bar – 2602 N. Clark St.
  (Lincoln Park)
NEAR NORTH WINE BARS
Juicy Wine Co. – 694 N. Milwaukee Ave.
Bin 36 – 339 N. Dearborn St.
Third Coast Café & Wine Bar –
  1260 N. Dearborn St.

TRIVIA   Now closed, what was Chicago's first wine bar?

NOTES   _____

_____

_____

_____

_____

ANSWER: *Le Bastille, at 21 W. Superior.*

WEEDS TAVERN

1555 N. Dayton St. (1600N, 850W)
Chicago, IL 60622
(312) 943-7815

Website	www.myspace.com/weeds_chicago
Neighborhood	SoNo (South of North Avenue)
Open 'til & Cover	2am (3am Sat), under $10 Sat night
Drinks	¡Tequila!, Jägermeister, bottled beer
Food	Only when visited by the Tamale Guy
Music	Live music (Sat), Slam Poetry (Mon)
Bar Type	Dive Bar, Neighborhood Tavern

The curious history of Weeds Tavern dates back to 1928 when it was a speakeasy known as Flisser Anton Soft Drinks. Not much is known about the place following Prohibition, but Weeds Tavern was established in 1964 and originally called the Fifteen 55 Club for its address. Current ownership took over in 1985 and cleaned it up. (Weeds has also benefited from the redevelopment—i.e., leveling—of the nearby Cabrini Green housing project.) "I think we're the only normal bar in Chicago," claims head bartender and artist-in-residence, Sergio Mayora, just as crazy people often describe themselves as the "only sane ones." Upon walking into Weeds, one is greeted by a wooden bust of Sergio holding a bottle of Cuervo Tequila (his favorite), free shots of which are often passed out if you're new to the bar, if you're an old regular, or if Sergio's tipsy. Beyond the infamous bust, you'll find a plethora of bras and panties hanging from the ceiling, a holdover from Underwear Night held many *moons* ago. An intriguing variety of bands play on Saturday night, usually with a single-digit cover charge (if one is charged at all). Monday is Free Your Mind Poetry Night, complete with thought-provoking subjects and ribald language, hosted by "G. Man" Gregorio Gomez in the slam poetry tradition started by Marc Smith in 1987 at Green Mill (p. 76). Even Sergio performs. Patrons also play pool and cornhole (Chicago-ese for bean bag toss) in the backyard beer garden.

NEARBY   Sully's House Tap Room – 1501 N. Dayton St.
Joe's Sports Bar – 940 W. Weed St.
Hogs & Honeys – 901 W. Weed St.

SIMILAR   **LEGENDARY DIVE BARS**
Billy Goat Tavern – 430 N. Michigan Ave.
Old Town Ale House – 219 W. North Ave.
Weeds Tavern – 1555 N. Dayton St.
ALTERNATIVE PERFORMANCE VENUES
Mutiny – 2428 N. Western Ave.
Gallery Cabaret – 2020 N. Oakley Ave.
Uncommon Ground – 3800 N. Clark St.

TRIVIA   In what state was cornhole invented?

NOTES   _____
_____
_____
_____
_____
_____
_____
_____

ANSWER: Ohio.

WHIRLAWAY

3224 W. Fullerton Ave. (2400N, 3200W)
Chicago, IL 60647
(773) 276-6809

Website	www.whirlaway.net
Neighborhood	Logan Square
Open 'til & Cover	2am (3am Sat); never a cover
Drinks	40 bottled beers, Margaritas
Food	If you're lucky, Maria brings in food
Music	Very good, lots of local indie music
Bar Type	Neighborhood Tavern

Just as Bucktown and Wicker Park were the trendy Bohemian neighborhoods of the '90s, Humboldt Park and Logan Square have taken the mantle this decade. Neighborhood taverns like Whirlaway not only trudged along through 40 years of urban decay but are also gaining a new-found popularity. In this case, it's thanks to the proprietress extraordinaire, Maria. The bar dates back to the mid-1940s and was named after the horse Whirlaway who won the Triple Crown in 1941. The previous owner placed a bet on Whirlaway and opened the bar with his winnings. Whirlaway (the bar) was purchased in 1980 by Maria Jaimes and her husband Sergio. Even with a recent renovation that saw the departure of the tiny pool table, the tavern still features the original tin ceiling and wooden bar. Maria is loved far and wide because she remembers your name, looks after you, and calls the boys *niño*. For the birthdays of regulars, she also serves homemade cakes, quesadillas, or lasagna after playing *Birthday* by the Beatles and a delivering a personal serenade of *Happy Birthday*. A complimentary shot of Jameson might even be thrown into the mix. Whirlaway is as fixated on the Cubs, without the typical sports bar crowd, as they are on politics, with election nights being a big draws. Whirlaway also features board games, with *Boggle* being surprisingly popular (probably because Maria will take on and beat patrons when business is slow). Whirlaway may not be as big as other pubs in the area, but it has the biggest heart.

NEARBY   The Burlington – 3425 W. Fullerton Ave.
            Weegee's Lounge – 3659 W. Armitage Ave.
            Two Way Lounge – 2928 W. Fullerton Ave.

SIMILAR   **LOGAN SQUARE CLASSICS**
            Bob Inn – 2609 W. Fullerton Ave.
            Rosa's Lounge – 3420 W. Armitage Ave.
            Mutiny – 2428 N. Western Ave.
            MORE LOGAN SQUARE NEW-SCHOOL
            Whistler – 2421 N. Milwaukee Ave.
            Green Eye Lounge – 2403 W. Homer St.
            Dunlay's on the Square – 3137 W. Logan Blvd.

TRIVIA   What is the statue in the center of Logan
            Square?

NOTES   _____

            _____

            _____

            _____

            _____

            _____

            _____

ANSWER: *The Illinois Centennial Memorial.*

WISE FOOLS PUB

2270 N. Lincoln Ave. (2300N, 700W)
Chicago, IL 60614
(773) 348-8899

Website	www.wisefoolspub.com
Neighborhood	Lincoln Park
Open 'til & Cover	2am (3am Sat); $5–10 cover
Drinks	75 beers, with nightly $1–3 specials
Food	Aladdin Falafel House next door
Music	Live rock & covers on most nights
Bar Type	Music Venue, Cocktail Lounge

Wise Fools Pub has a long, interesting history that has played out in three acts. Act I: Wise Fools Pub opens in 1968 and becomes one of the North Side's most popular blues clubs, particularly once David Ungeleider takes over in 1972 and invites blues legends from South Side clubs like Theresa's (p. 222), such as Muddy Waters, Howlin' Wolf, and Jimmy Dawkins. George Thorogood made his first Chicago appearance at Wise Fools Pub, and Otis Rush and Mighty Joe Young both recorded live albums here. Act II: Ungeleider sells his pub in 1993, new ownership renames it Waterloo Tavern and features mainly local rock and cover bands to appeal to the increasing post-frat weekend traffic along Lincoln Avenue. Act III: Waterloo is sold in 2001 and transformed once again into Wise Fools Pub by Mike and Dan Cordis. Dan worked at Waterloo and got the idea for the rebirth of Wise Fools Pub from neighborhood locals and former owner Ungeleider himself, who gave his blessing to the new Fools opening night, accompanied by music from bluesman Son Seals. As a postscript, Wise Fools Pub is now owned by Chris Perry and Big Bill Vance, who renovated Wise Fools Pub in 2007 into a hybrid between Waterloo Tavern and the original, with a new sound system. Jam bands and cover bands are now mainly featured, in addition to a large beer selection, darts, pool, Golden Tee, and a loungy atmosphere.

NEARBY	John Barleycorn Memorial Pub – 658 W. Belden Ave. Halligan Bar – 2274 N. Lincoln Ave. Kelsey's – 2265 N. Lincoln Ave.
SIMILAR	**INTIMATE ROCK CLUBS** Elbo Room – 2871 N. Lincoln Ave. Beat Kitchen – 2100 W. Belmont Ave. Silvie's Lounge – 1902 W. Irving Park Rd. **LINCOLN PARK LOUNGES** Marquee Lounge – 1973 N. Halsted St. Tonic Room – 2447 N. Halsted St. Soirée Bar Bistro – 2438 N. Lincoln Ave.
TRIVIA	What other Lincoln Park blues legend opened in 1968?
NOTES	_____ _____ _____ _____ _____ _____

WOODLAWN TAP

1172 E. 55th St. (5500S, 1100E)
Chicago, IL 60615
(773) 643-5516

Website	None
Neighborhood	Hyde Park
Open 'til & Cover	2am (3am Sat); never a cover
Drinks	Beer and booze at student prices
Food	Cheap-but-good pub grub
Music	Good juke and free Sunday night jazz
Bar Type	Neighborhood Tavern, College Bar

Jimmy Wilson ran what he called the Woodlawn Tap, but what everyone else called Jimmy's—the last of the lively 55th Street bar scene. Following brief stints working for Drexel Bank and bartending at nearby University Tap (now gone), Wilson ran Woodlawn Tap from 1948 until his death in 1999. During his reign, Jimmy catered to all races, ethnicities, classes, and social groups, including University of Chicago faculty and staff, construction workers, and businessmen. Famous patrons include Pulitzer Prize winner Saul Bellow (as both U of C student and professor) and anthropologist Margaret Mead. Even the Welsh poet Dylan Thomas stopped by not once, but three times *on the same day*, between U of C speaking engagements. Jimmy was so loved that the University of Chicago itself recognized him on his 70th birthday, with a proclamation naming him an honorary post-doctoral alumnus for providing fond memories to decades of U of C students. If you appreciate the 2008 Illinois Smoking Ban, you can thank the Woodlawn Tap. The Environmental Protection Agency surveyed air quality in Chicago restaurants and bars and found the Woodlawn Tap to be the worst. Patrons had always claimed that the bar was smoky, but no one realized that it was equivalent to breathing in the air following a volcanic eruption. The air has been cleared and Jimmy's legend lives on under the ownership of Jim and Bill Callahan.

NEARBY	The Cove – 1750 E. 55th St.
	Seven Ten – 1055 E. 55th St.
	New Checkerboard Lounge – 5201 S. Harper Ct.
SIMILAR	**WRITER HANGOUTS**
	Billy Goat Tavern – 430 N. Lower Michigan Ave.
	Rainbo Club – 1150 N. Damen Ave.
	Charleston – 2076 N. Hoyne Ave.
	CLASSIC COLLEGE PUBS
	Hawkeye's – 1458 W. Taylor St. (UIC)
	Kelly's Pub – 949 W. Webster Ave. (DePaul)
	Hamilton's – 6341 N. Broadway (Loyola)
TRIVIA	What major beer label did Jimmy refuse to sell even after Harry Caray's personal request?

NOTES

_____

_____

_____

_____

_____

_____

_____

ANSWER: Budweiser.

YAK-ZIES ON CLARK

3710 N. Clark St. (3700N, 1200W)
Chicago, IL 60613
(773) 525-9200

Website	www.yakzies.com
Neighborhood	Wrigleyville
Open 'til & Cover	2am (3am Sat); never a cover
Drinks	Seven beers on tap
Food	Mild, hot, and "Oh My Gosh" wings
Music	The roar of the crowd across the street
Bar Type	Sports Bar, Neighborhood Tavern

Yak-zies on Clark dates back to 1990, but the story begins when Ken Miller opened the original, late-night, subterranean Yak-zies on Diversey in 1966, in a brownstone next to the landmark Brewster Apartments (Charlie Chaplin lived in the penthouse in 1915). "Yak-zies" comes from Miller's son mimicking his father saying, *Jak sie masz?* or, "Hello, how are you?" in Polish. The logo depicts the sun rising over Lake Michigan, nursing a hangover with an icepack—an uncanny prediction of what will happen to you after a night at Yak-zies. This original location also inspired the opening scene of David Mamet's play, *Sexual Perversity in Chicago*, and the film *About Last Night*. Ken Miller passed on in 2007 and, because of a licensing glitch, the Diversey location was closed for almost two years but re-opened in 2009. Yak-zies on Clark is now run by Miller's son-in-law, Joe Spagnoli, and is a Wrigleyville staple with its "Tang Peeza" and buffalo wings made from the original recipe of the Anchor Bar in Buffalo, NY. If you don't have tickets for the Cubs across the street, you can watch them here on 15 TVs and four big screens. The spacious beer garden is also a hit in warm weather. As for the crowd, if you wear a green sweatshirt, Cubs hat, and black track pants, there will be someone here dressed exactly like you. An additional Yak-zies is in Pompano Beach, Florida, for your "off-season."

NEARBY   Trace – 3714 N. Clark St.
Raw Bar & Grill – 3720 N. Clark St.
Full Schilling Public House – 3728 N. Clark St.

SIMILAR   **BEST WINGS IN CHICAGOLAND**
Buffalo Wild Wings – 2464 N. Lincoln Ave.
Chicago Joe's – 812 Clark St. (Evanston)
Gators Wing Shack – 1719 Rand Rd. (Palatine)
BEST SPOTS FOR CUBS OPENING DAY
    PRE-GAMING
Cubby Bear – 1059 W. Addison St.
Murphy's Bleachers – 3655 N. Sheffield Ave.
Goose Island Wrigleyville – 3535 N. Clark St.

TRIVIA   Who was burned, shot, dismembered, and
killed in the hallway of the adjacent Brewster
Apartments?

NOTES   _____

              _____

              _____

              _____

              _____

ZEBRA LOUNGE

1220 N. State Pkwy. (1200N, 0W)
Chicago, IL 60610
(312) 642-5140

Website	None
Neighborhood	Gold Coast
Open 'til & Cover	2am (3am Sat); never a cover
Drinks	Cocktails, abbreviated beer list
Food	Wooden bowls full of "bar mix"
Music	Live piano
Bar Type	Piano Lounge, Cocktail Lounge

What Zebra Lounge lacks in space, it makes up for in character. Its unlikely location is a small room on the first floor of Canterbury Courts, a vintage apartment building used to house students from the University of Illinois at Chicago. Zebra Lounge dates back to the day Prohibition ended in 1933, its current name inspired by a small lounge bar in a New York hotel, circa 1960. A zebra-striped awning over the sidewalk begins the animal print motif, which continues inside with zebra skins, "striped" mirrors behind the bar, and the namesake creature painted upon the mirrored wall. If you want a seat, get there before 10pm and snag a seat at the crescent-shaped booth, or pull up a stool at the tiny bar along the western wall. Since the mid-'60s, Tommy Oman has entertained multi-generational lounge lizards here on his two-tier synthesizer with stylized versions of torch songs and piano standards (he formerly performed with Barry Manilow at the Croyden Hotel). This curious watering hole is a pleasant oasis away from the urban lechery just around the corner that is the Division Street scene. Zebra Lounge is also the location every March, July, and November of the Dil Pickle Club [sic], a program of spoken word, music, and performance art. The idea was resurrected by editors from *Lumpen* and *Stop Smiling* magazines and based on the activist "Wobbly" Jack Jones's original club that ran from 1914 to 1933.

NEARBY	Mother's, The Original – 26 W. Division St.
	Butch McGuire's – 20 W. Division St.
	Hangge Uppe – 14 W. Elm St.
SIMILAR	**PIANO BARS**
	Redhead Piano Bar – 16 W. Ontario St.
	Underground Wonder Bar – 10 E. Walton St.
	Davenport's – 1383 N. Milwaukee Ave.
	SWANKY HOTEL LOUNGES
	Pump Room – 1301 N. State (Ambassador East)
	Coq d'Or – 140 E. Walton St. (Drake Hotel)
	Crimson Lounge – 333 N. Dearborn (Hotel Sax)
TRIVIA	What nearby bar was also named after a New York Tavern?
NOTES	_____
	_____
	_____
	_____
	_____
	_____
	_____

ANSWER: *PJ Clarke's.*

HISTORIC SUBURBAN TAVERNS

The Best of the Chicago Suburbs

COUNTRY HOUSE

241 W. 55th St.
Clarendon Hills, IL 60559
(630) 325-1444

Website	www.burgerone.com
Neighborhood	Western Suburbs
Open 'til & Cover	11pm (1am Fri/Sat); never a cover
Drinks	Eight beers on tap, more in bottles
Food	Award-winning burgers
Music	Jukebox with classic rock & country
Bar Type	Roadhouse, Haunted

Located in a lesser-known western suburb, this two-story, wood-frame roadhouse was built by Emil Kobel in 1922. During Prohibition, Kobel's roadhouse remained open as a grocery store and restaurant, discreetly serving booze to regulars. Kobel retired in 1957 and sold the place to Richard Montanelli, a decorated World War II bomber pilot. Area resident David Regnery, then purchased the joint in 1974 and re-christened it Country House. Since then, additional suburban locations have opened in Lisle (1985) and Geneva (1996). During renovations in the mid-'70s, several shutters opened by themselves and Chicago's famous ghost hunter Richard Crowe was summoned to investigate. The two psychics he brought in felt the presence of a young blonde woman who died in the 1950s of abdominal injuries. Sure enough, the previous owner recalled the story of Marion who had stopped in just before driving her car into a tree in an apparent suicide. The waitstaff today claims they can smell her perfume and that she beckons young men on the street from the second floor, dressed in ghostly white. Most suspicious activity happens after hours, so as not to disturb you from enjoying their top-rated, half-pound burgers. The bar offers 30 beers in total and ten wines under $30. The barroom features a stone fireplace below a stuffed boar's head, and people shuck shells from free peanuts onto the old wooden floor.

NEARBY Uptown – 12 W. Burlington Ave. (Westmont)
Tracy's Tavern – 401 55th St. (Clarendon Hills)
Ballydoyle Pub – 5157 Main St. (Downer's Grove)

SIMILAR **SUBURBAN BURGER PUBS**
Hackney's – 1241 Harms Rd. (Glenview)
Alfie's Inn – 425 Roosevelt Rd. (Glen Ellyn)
Bristol Tap – 46 N. Cannonball Tr. (Bristol)
SUBURBAN ROADHOUSES
Village Tavern – 135 Old McHenry (Long Grove)
Morrison Roadhouse – 7355 N. Harlem Ave.
  (Niles)
Billy's Roadhouse – 40W484 Rt. 64 (St. Charles)

TRIVIA Clarendon Hills was named after a suburb of
what city?

NOTES _____

_____

_____

_____

_____

_____

ANSWER: Boston.

HACKNEY'S

1241 Harms Rd.
Glenview, IL 60025
(847) 724-5577

Website	www.hackneys.net
Neighborhood	Northern Suburbs
Open 'til & Cover	10pm daily; never a cover
Drinks	Solid selection on tap, cocktails
Food	Hackneyburgers, black rye, onion loaf
Music	The sizzling sound of burgers grilling
Bar Type	Neighborhood Tavern

Hackney's isn't the oldest restaurant or pub in the area, but it is one of the best known, replicating the inimitable Hackneyburgers, inviting pub atmosphere, and pleasant beer garden at all six of their Chicagoland locations. The Printers Row location in Chicago is the most recent addition, but the original Harms Road location is the most notable and historic. Jim and Kitz Masterson opened Hackney's in 1939, using recipes from their aunt and uncle, Bebe and Jack Hackney, who had served hamburgers and beer on the back porch of their house in Glenview in the 1920s, then added a small, four-seater bar in their home following the end of Prohibition. Today, the torch has been passed to the third generation with Ed and Jim Hebson, who opened the two most recent Hackney's installments. The Hackneyburger is a half-pound of fresh, unfrozen ground beef, grilled and served on homemade dark rye or a fresh baked bun. It's quite juicy so you'll probably want to eat it with knife and fork, and it's won so many awards, the novelty's worn off. The Bleu Cheese Burger and Inside Out Burger (with cheddar and bacon cooked right into the meat) are also hits. Up to five tons of beef are used for these Hackneyburgers every week. The award-winning onion loaf (like a brick of fried onions), French Dip, and fried fish on Fridays are all laudable, non-burger options, and the leafy beer garden facing Harms Woods Forest Preserve is highly sought after in summer.

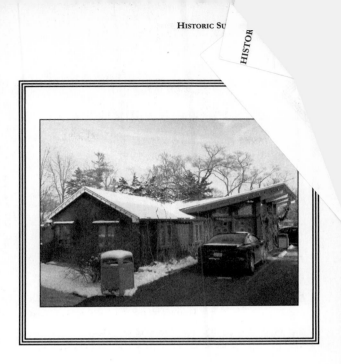

NEARBY	Meier's Tavern – 235 E. Lake Ave. (Glenview)
	EJ's Place – 10027 Skokie Blvd. (Skokie)
	Seul's Tavern & Grill – 1735 Orchard Ln.
	(Northfield)
SIMILAR	**SUBURBAN BURGER PUBS**
	Country House – 241 W. 55th St.
	(Clarendon Hills)
	Jake Moran's – 57 S. Lake St. (Mundelein)
	Goldyburgers – 7316 Circle Ave. (Forest Park)
	CHICAGOLAND TAVERN CHAINS
	Bar Louie (fifty-one locations)
	Billy Goat Tavern (eight locations)
	John Barleycorn's (four locations)
TRIVIA	Where was the first hamburger served in the U.S.?
NOTES	_____
	_____
	_____
	_____
	_____

ANSWER: At Louis Lunch, New Haven, CT (1895).

HALA KAHIKI

2834 River Rd.
River Grove, IL 60171
(708) 456-3222

Website	www.hala-kahiki.com
Neighborhood	Collar Suburb
Open 'til & Cover	2am (3am Sat); never a cover
Drinks	Over 100 tropical drinks
Food	Free pretzels, fruit in your cocktail
Music	Don Ho & the Rat Pack, softly played
Bar Type	Tiki Bar (extraordinaire)

Now that Cyril's House of Tiki, Rock-a-Tiki, and Prodigal Son have passed into the mists of time (the latter of which burned down after Free Bacon Night), one can fully appreciate Hala Kahiki—a magical tiki experience. It didn't start that way. Stanley and Rose Sacharski bought a wood-paneled, Dillinger-era tavern in 1965. After experimenting with bamboo, Stanley went whole-hog tropical. "Proper attire required," reads the sign as you walk in, but only pertains to men: no hats, cut-offs, tank tops, or sleeveless shirts. Around the corner is the bar, followed by three additional rooms outfitted in a Polynesian explosion: a thatched bar overhang, walls lined with bamboo, puffer fish lights, and a waitstaff bedecked in Hawaiian shirts and sarongs. The beer garden offers a Witco fountain, seasonal displays, and cabanas for relaxation in summer and smokers' refuge in winter. Hala Kahiki serves Mai Tais, Piña Coladas, and Zombies, along with two-person cocktails, rum daiquiris, martinis, and drinks made from cream, coffee, and ice cream— more than 100 concoctions in all. The gift shop all the way in the back is where you can purchase a grass skirt and lei, ceramic panda beverage holder, and a Brady Bunch–like tiki idol. If you're hungry or need to sober up, grab a dog at nearby Gene & Jude's Red Hot Stand (2720 River Rd.) afterwards. *Okole maluna!* (Hawaiian for "bottoms up.")

NEARBY	Totu Café – 2300 River Rd.
	D&J Tap – 9743 Franklin Ave.
	Sporty's – 1908 N. 5th Ave.
SIMILAR	**CHICAGO TIKI ROOMS**
	Bottom Lounge – 1375 W. Lake St.
	Holiday Club – 4000 N. Sheridan Rd.
	Trader Vic's – 1030 N. State St.
	TOP U.S. TIKI BARS
	Tonga Room – 950 Mason St. (San Francisco)
	Mai Kai – 3599 N. Federal Hwy. (Ft. Lauderdale)
	Forbidden Island – 1304 Lincoln Ave. (Alameda)
TRIVIA	What does *Hala Kahiki* mean?

NOTES

_____

_____

_____

_____

_____

_____

_____

ANSWER: *"House of Pineapple" in Hawaiian, the pineapple being symbolic of hospitality.*

VILLAGE TAVERN

135 N. Old McHenry Rd.
Long Grove, IL 60047
(847) 634-3117

Website	www.villagetavernoflonggrove.com
Neighborhood	Far Northwest Suburbs
Open 'til & Cover	9pm (10pm Sat), closed Tue; no cover
Drinks	14 wines under $30, champagne
Food	1/2 lb. Black Angus burgers, steaks
Music	Roger Pauly's Dixieland Jazz, nightly
Bar Type	Neighborhood Tavern, Restaurant

Originally named for its surfeit of oak trees, Long Grove was first settled in 1838 by Germans from Alsace & Lorraine (now France). The Village Tavern was established in 1849 in what was John Zimmer's Wagon Shop, and has continuously operated since that time—making it the oldest tavern in the Chicagoland area and one of the country's 20 oldest. The Village Tavern is now owned by Chip and Mary Ann Ullrich, who maintain its rustic authenticity, particularly with its décor of old photographs and antiques for sale. The centerpiece of the pub is a 35-foot mahogany bar that survived the McCormick Place Fire of January 16, 1961. The spacious dining room features a home-cooked menu highlighted by the half-pound Black Angus burger, all-you-can-eat broasted chicken on Wednesdays, all-you-can-eat fish fry on Fridays, and Prime Rib on Saturdays. Buffalo wings, sandwiches, a few salads, hand-cut steaks, chops, and fish are also available, as is a brunch buffet every Sunday from 9am to noon. Live music is featured every night starting around 5pm, mostly by Roger Pauly's Dixieland jazz band, the RJ Express. The crowd consists primarily of an older suburban crowd, except for the busloads of tourists that come to shop in Long Grove's quaint nineteenth-century downtown and to experience a Victorian Christmas or the springtime Chocolate Fest. All of the above, plus restrictive alcohol licensing, makes the Village Tavern the only bar in town.

NEARBY   Kathy's Lakeside – 24238 N. Lakeside Dr.
             (Lake Zurich)
             Irish Mill – 26592 N. Route 83 (Mundelein)
             Old Munich Inn – 582 N. Milwaukee Ave.
             (Wheeling)

SIMILAR **OLDEST SUBURBAN TAVERNS**
             Country House – Clarendon Hills (1922)
             Deer Path Inn – Lake Forest (1929)
             Meier's Tavern – Glenview (1933)
             OLDEST PUBS IN THE UNITED STATES
             White Horse Tavern – Providence, RI (1673)
             Middleton's Tavern – Annapolis, MD (1750)
             Pirate's House – Savannah, GA (1753)

TRIVIA   What is the oldest tavern in the city of
             Chicago?

NOTES   _____

             _____

             _____

             _____

             _____

ANSWER: Schaller's Pump (1881).

WALTER PAYTON'S ROUNDHOUSE

205 N. Broadway (Route 25)
Aurora, IL 60505
(630) 264-BREW (2739)

Website	www.walterpaytonsroundhouse.com
Neighborhood	Far West Suburbs
Open 'til & Cover	10pm (11pm Fri/Sat); never a cover
Drinks	3 World Beer Cup winners and more
Food	Steaks, seafood, pasta, jambalaya
Music	Rock cover bands in the gazebo
Bar Type	Brew Pub, Historical Landmark

In 1856, the Chicago Burlington & Quincy Railroad built the first roundhouse in Aurora, the second largest city in Illinois, to house and repair steam locomotives. The imposing structure is 70,000 square feet in size with 18-foot walls of limestone. Locomotives yielded to Zephyrs, which yielded to cars, causing the roundhouse to close in 1974 and stand vacant for 20 years, reflecting the urban decay surrounding it. That's when the Pride of the Chicago Bears and Hall of Fame running back #34 Walter Payton came to the rescue and purchased the structure with investors for $10, plus the millions of dollars needed to rehab it. After a year of renovation, Walter Payton's Roundhouse opened in 1996. The result is an adult amusement complex near the banks of the Fox River, adjacent to the last station on Metra's Burlington North Santa Fe line. You can enjoy a steak in the restaurant and wash it down with an array of award-winning, handcrafted ales brewed on the premises. You can pay homage to "Sweetness" in the Walter Payton museum, head to the comedy club, listen to bands in the courtyard, and have a nightcap at the cognac bar, originally built for the Anheuser-Busch booth at the World's Columbian Exposition in 1893. In 1999, the National Trust awarded Roundhouse and City of Aurora the *National Preservation Honor* for their stunning achievement.

NEARBY	Doug's Rockhouse – 333 E. Indian Tr. (Aurora)
	Tavern on the Fox – 24 N. Broadway (Aurora)
	Muddy Duck Inn – 1 S. Stolp Ave. (Aurora)
SIMILAR	**NEW LIFE FOR AN OLD LANDMARK**
	Motel Bar – 600 W. Chicago Ave. (Montgomery Ward)
	Lockwood – 17 E. Monroe St. (Palmer House)
	Paramount Room – 415 N. Milwaukee Ave. (speakeasy)
	CHICAGOLAND BREW PUBS
	Goose Island Brew Pub – 1800 N. Clybourn Ave.
	Piece – 1927 W. North Ave.
	Flatlander's – 200 Village Green (Lincolnshire)
TRIVIA	What famous artwork at the Roundhouse depicts bears illustrating every human emotion?

NOTES _____

_____

_____

_____

_____

ANSWER: The Bear Dance, by William Holbrook Beard.

⚜

HONORABLE MENTION

House of Glunz
The Glunz Family has done more to advance the enjoyment of intoxicants in Chicago than any other over the past 120 years.

HOUSE OF GLUNZ

1206 N. Wells St. (1200N, 200W)
Chicago, IL 60610
(312) 642-3000

Website	thehouseofglunz.com
Neighborhood	Old Town
Open 'til & Cover	10am–8pm M–F (7pm Sat, 5pm Sun)
Drinks	Wine tastings every Saturday at 2pm
Food	Caviar, cheese, and chocolate for sale
Music	The soft shuffling of feet
Bar Type	Wine Store with Tasting Room

The oldest, continuously family-owned enterprise in Chicago is not a bar, corporation, or even a political machine, but rather a wine shop. Founded in 1888 by Louis Glunz, the House of Glunz has served as a wine wholesaler, beer distributor, tavern before Prohibition, and a wine shop today. Following the World's Columbian Exposition of 1893, Glunz was the first to bottle and distribute Schlitz, making spin-off Louis Glunz Beer the country's oldest beer distributor. In the beginning, Glunz sold cask wine and spirits to those picking up their orders by horse-drawn carriage. On their 75th anniversary in 1963, Glunz opened a wine museum adjacent to the shop that now serves as a tasting room every Saturday from 2pm to 6pm. In the late '70s, House of Glunz was the first in town to promote California wines as rivals to their French counterparts—after all, California did save the global wine industry from phylloxera in the late nineteenth century... There were hard times however: House of Glunz barely survived Prohibition (served soft drinks à la Berghoff, p. 2) and two decades of urban decay in the '70s and '80s. Today, customers are still buzzed in and the mother/son duo of Barbara Glunz-Donovan and Christopher Donovan keep the family tradition alive with their handpicked selection and unsurpassed knowledge of wine. The extended Glunz family opened a fortified small-batch winery in Grayslake in 1992 and a German bierstube, Glunz Bavarian Haus, in North Center in 2003.

NEARBY   Saluki Bar & Grill – 1208 N. Wells St.
              Old Town Pub – 1339 N. Wells St.
              Suite Lounge – 1446 N. Wells St.

SIMILAR   **CHICAGO'S CLASSIC WINE SHOPS**
              Schaefer's – 9965 Gross Point Rd. (Skokie, 1936)
              Binny's Beverage Depot – 3000 N. Clark St.
                   (1947)
              DiCarlo's Armanetti – 515 N. Western Ave.
                   (1930s)
              CHICAGO'S TOP WINE BARS
              Webster's Wine Bar – 1480 W. Webster Ave.
              Bin 36 – 339 N. Dearborn St. (Marina City)
              DOC Wine Bar – 2602 N. Clark St.

TRIVIA   What culture is credited with inventing wine?

NOTES   _____

              _____

              _____

              _____

              _____

              _____

ANSWER: The Mesopotamians in 6,000 B.C. (est.).

Bars We Miss the Most

*Historic Chicago Taverns
in Memoriam*

WOLF TAVERN

Located at Wolf Point
(Approximately 300N, 500W)
R.I.P. 1834

Neighborhood	Fulton River District
Drinks	Gin, whiskey, rum, wine, brandy
Food	Beef and poultry
Music	Unknown (probably bawdy ballads)
Bar Type	Neighborhood Tavern, Traveler's Inn

Chicago's first tavern license was granted on December 8, 1829, to Archibald "Billy" Caldwell, the son of an Irish colonel and a Potawatomi maiden. Known as Sauganash ("Englishman") amongst the tribe, Caldwell saved his friend James Kinzie from the Fort Dearborn Massacre in 1812. The two later built a log inn in 1823 that became Wolf Tavern in 1829, just west of Chicago River, "a few rods" north of the main branch and just south of the Kinzie Street bridge today. This was the epicenter of early *Chickagou* (Potawatomi for "smelly onion") for about 20 years. Two competing stories explain the naming of Wolf Tavern: Either it was named after Potawatomi chief Alexander Robinson's nephew, known as Mo-a-way ("Wolf"); or after the local legend of Elijah Wentworth, Sr., who took over Wolf Tavern in 1830, killing a wolf in his meat room "alone and unaided." We do know that wolves were common in this area—initially called The Forks and then Wolf Point. The Wolf Tavern also witnessed Chicago's first criminal act around 1830. A man stole $34 from a fellow boarder, was arrested and tried in the Wolf Tavern. He was found guilty when the money was discovered in his sock, and then disappeared following release on a nominal bail. Across the river from Wolf Tavern, Samuel Miller received a license in 1831 for Miller House, Chicago's second tavern. Mark Beaubien opened his lively pub that same year at Lake & Market streets, and named it Sauganash Tavern, after Billy Caldwell. James Kinzie went on to found the Green Tree Tavern in 1833.

The site of Wolf Tavern—where Chicago itself began—
is now occupied by the Riverbend Condominiums.

NEARBY   Miller House –
  Kingsbury Ave. & Mart Center Dr.
  Sauganash Tavern –
  Lake & Market (now Wacker Dr.)
  Green Tree Tavern – Lake St. & Canal St.

SIMILAR   **OLDEST TAVERN LEGACIES**
  Schaller's Pump – 3714 S. Halsted St.
  Marge's Still – 1758 N. Sedgwick St.
  17 West at the Berghoff – 17 W. Adams St.
  TODAY'S WOLF POINT TAVERNS
  Coogan's Riverside Saloon – 180 N. Wacker Dr.
  Paramount Room – 415 N. Milwaukee Ave.
  Emmit's Irish Pub – 495 N. Milwaukee Ave.

TRIVIA   When was the City of Chicago incorporated?

ANSWER: *March 4, 1837.*

THERESA'S LOUNGE

4801 S. Indiana Ave. (4800S, 200E)
Chicago, IL 60615
R.I.P. 1983

Neighborhood	Bronzeville
Drinks	Bottled beer and booze
Food	Bags of chips, only if you brought 'em
Music	Live blues, Fri–Mon
Bar Type	Blues Club, Dive Bar

Before there were clubs like B.L.U.E.S., Rosa's Lounge, and Buddy Guy's Legends, there were humble South Side joints that helped define Chicago as the blues capital of the world. Beginning at the end of World War II, rural blacks from the Delta Region of Northwestern Mississippi descended upon Chi-town in search of work in the steel mills. Life was hard, leading many to adapt their native Delta Blues into an urban form of music that reflected their angst with an amplified edge. A series of bars opened up on the South Side, showcasing this new music, including Theresa's Lounge. Within the tight confines of an apartment building's basement, Theresa Needham opened her tavern in December 1949. Junior Wells led the house band with auto-mechanic-by-day Buddy Guy on lead guitar. These and other bluesmen showcased the Chicago style of blues for a cover charge of not more than $2. Theresa's attracted a middle-aged, working class crowd from the tough surrounding neighborhood. The appeal of her club reached global proportions as time wore on, with more and more becoming aware of the caliber of music offered regularly there. Unfortunately, so that her landlord could qualify for government rental subsidies, Theresa's lease was terminated to make way for a laundry room. Theresa moved but called it quits within three years after an impressive run of 33 years. In recognition of her legacy, Theresa Needham became only one of two non-performers voted into the prestigious Blues Foundation Hall of Fame in 2001, nine years after her passing.

The apartment building once housing Theresa's
now just houses apartments.

NEARBY   Cove Lounge – 1750 E. 55th St.

Woodlawn Tap – 1172 E. 55th St.

Mr. T's Lounge – 3528 S. Indiana Ave.

SIMILAR   **BEST SOUTH SIDE BLUES**

Buddy Guy's Legends – 754 S. Wabash Ave.

New Checkerboard Lounge – 5201 S. Harper Ct.

Lee's Unleaded Blues –

7401 S. South Chicago Ave.

BEST NORTH SIDE BLUES

Rosa's Lounge – 3420 W. Armitage Ave.

B.L.U.E.S. – 2548 N. Halsted St.

Kingston Mines – 2548 N. Halsted St.

TRIVIA   What bluesman got his start at Theresa's at age 16?

PLAYBOY CLUB

116 E. Walton St. (950N, 100E)
Chicago, IL 60611
R.I.P. 1986

Neighborhood	Gold Coast
Drinks	Cocktails, exorbitantly priced at $1.50
Food	Steaks and salads
Music	Mel Torme, Barbara Streisand, jazz
Bar Type	Cocktail Lounge, Jazz Club

February 29, 1960, was a historic day for Chicago and the world. *Playboy* magazine founder and Hyde Park native Hugh Hefner opened the world's first Playboy Club, a swanky nightclub that introduced the Playboy Bunnies. Rather than posing nude, these Bunnies served keyholder members in the style of the old gaslight clubs, but with satin corsets, bunny ears, and fluffy white tails. As VIPs of the club, keyholders ($50 for residents and $25 for out-of-towners) could enter the club anytime and indulge in music, alcohol, and nubile women. Each of the club's four floors was designed as a separate room in a mythical bachelor pad: Playroom, Penthouse, Library, and Living Room. Though obvious objects of desire, all Bunnies were under strict orders enforced by the Willmark Detective Agency: Avoid dating members and giving out your phone number, or face expulsion from "the hutch." The Bunny costume was so notable that it became the first service uniform registered by the United States Patent Office. This flagship Playboy Club location was the first of 40, each referred to by *Newsweek* as a "Disneyland for adults." The Chicago Playboy Club was also a strategic addition to the Magnificent Mile hotel bar district, and helped solidify the greater Rush and Division Street area as one of the most happening areas in the country in the 1960s. The original Chicago location enjoyed a long and successful run, but closed in 1986. The last U.S. Playboy Club closed in 1988 in Lansing, Michigan, and the last international club closed in 1991. After 31 years, the Playboy Club was no more.

The pink granite One Magnificent Mile building stands between Walton Place and Oak Street where the Playboy Club once stood.

NEARBY	Coq d'Or – 140 E. Walton St. (Drake Hotel)
	Signature Lounge – 875 N. Michigan Ave., 96th Fl.
	Seasons Bar – 120 E. Delaware Pl. (Four Seasons)
SIMILAR	**1960s NIGHTLIFE, REVISITED**
	Gaslight Club – Hilton Chicago O'Hare Airport
	Pump Room – 1301 N. State Pkwy.
	BackRoom – 1007 N. Rush St.
	SWANKY DEPARTED LEGENDS
	Gold Star Sardine Bar – 680 N. Lake Shore Dr.
	Mister Kelly's – 1028 N. Rush St.
	London House – 360 N. Michigan Ave.
TRIVIA	Who was *Playboy* magazine's first centerfold?

LOUNGE AX

2438 N. Lincoln Ave. (2500N, 900W)
Chicago, IL 60614
R.I.P. 2000

Neighborhood	Lincoln Park
Drinks	A handful of beers on tap
Food	None, and that was a good thing
Music	The best indie bands of a generation
Bar Type	Music Venue, Neighborhood Tavern

Few things have caused as much anxiety in the Chicago live music scene as the closing of the legendary rock club Lounge Ax. After succumbing to intolerant complaints of neighbors, an unsympathetic liquor commissioner, and the blasé attitude of a new landlord, Lounge Ax shuttered its doors on January 15, 2000. Julie Adams and Sue Miller opened Lounge Ax in 1987 and its rise in popularity both paralleled and influenced alternative music itself. The club helped launch the career of many successful indie bands, including the Smashing Pumpkins, Liz Phair, Urge Overkill, The Replacements, Poi Dog Pondering, The Mekons, Yo La Tengo, The Drovers, Jesus Lizard, Naked Raygun, Neutral Milk Hotel, Sebadoh, Archers of Loaf, Superchunk, Old 97's, and Material Issue. The cover charge ranged between $5 and $10, and lines often stretched down Lincoln Avenue just like they do at the Vic Theater today (in between Brew & View nights). While it was a total dive, the dynamic female owners created a space that people loved, whether a band played or not. The interior of Lounge Ax was one long continuous space with a battered wooden bar and a crazy little stage in the back located under a leaky ceiling. Décor consisted of purple walls, a couch without legs, year-round Christmas lights, and Elvis paraphernalia—all of which added to Lounge Ax's Bohemian chic feel and complimented the music perfectly. There are many great places to see up-and-coming bands in Chicago today, but Lounge Ax was unique, and almost a decade after its closing, it's still sorely missed.

Soireé has replaced Gramercy as the second
successor to Lounge Ax.

NEARBY	Lincoln Station – 2432 N. Lincoln Ave.
	Clarke's Bar & Grill – 2445 N. Lincoln Ave.
	Hi-Tops – 2462 N. Lincoln Ave.
SIMILAR	**INDIE MUSIC HAVENS**
	Empty Bottle – 1035 N. Western Ave. (indie rock)
	Hideout – 1354 W. Wabansia Ave. (indie folk)
	Mutiny – 2428 N. Western Ave. (punk)
	DEPARTED LIVE MUSIC LEGENDS
	O'Banion's – 661 N. Clark St.
	Earl of Old Town – 1615 N. Wells St.
	Gaspar's – 3159 N. Southport Ave.
TRIVIA	Liz Phair shot her *Exile in Guyville* album cover in which bar's photo booth, exposed nipple and all?

RED LION PUB

2446 N. Lincoln Ave. (2500N, 900W)
Chicago, IL 60614
R.I.P. 2007

Neighborhood	Lincoln Park
Drinks	Pints of British ale and cider
Food	Shepherd's pie, fish & chips, rarebit
Music	Only the sounds of patrons, VCR films
Bar Type	English Pub, Dive Bar, Haunted

The structure housing the Red Lion Pub was built in 1882, eleven years after the Great Chicago Fire and seven years before the town of Lake View was annexed to Chicago in 1889. Across the street is the Biograph Theater, where John Dillinger was gunned down after being fingered by the Lady in Red. The building later hosted an upstairs gambling hall, a produce stand, laundry, typewriter assembly facility, and a head shop. A British chap, John Cordwell, rescued the building from Dirty Dan's in 1984. Red Lion Pub was chosen as the bar's name to honor one of the most common pub names in England (after "The Crown"). In his previous career as an architect, Cordwell was instrumental in creating Carl Sandburg Village, Presidential Towers, and the Blue Line "L." The Red Lion was quite well known for its apparitions, including a woman named Sharon who trapped women in the second floor restroom, a man killed over a gambling debt, a woman that died of measles when apartments were located upstairs, a mentally disabled woman known for her lavender perfume that also died here, and malicious former owner, "Dirty Dan" Danforth. Perhaps even creepier was the Chinese sumac or "stink tree" on the rooftop deck that seemed to grow out of the building itself. John Cordwell passed away in 1999 and his son, Colin, now owns the place. Colin initially planned to tear the building down to build a new version of the Red Lion with condos above, but is now planning to remodel and re-open soon. The ghosts should be pleased.

The Red Lion continues to stand vacant,
awaiting its destruction.

NEARBY   Lincoln Station – 2432 N. Lincoln Ave.

Soirée – 2438 N. Lincoln Ave.

Hi-Tops – 2462 N. Lincoln Ave.

SIMILAR   **TOP ANGLOPHILE PUBS**

Duke of Perth – 2913 N. Clark St. (Scottish)

Globe Pub – 1934 W. Irving Park Rd. (English)

Elephant & Castle – 111 W. Adams St. (English)

APPARITION CENTRAL

Excalibur Nightclub – 632 N. Dearborn St.

Gold Star Bar – 1755 W. Division St.

Ole St. Andrew's Inn – 5938 N. Broadway

TRIVIA   John Cordwell inspired "The Forger" in what
World War II movie?

ANSWER: The Great Escape (1963).

HISTORIC PUB CRAWLS

Have an Epic Night Out in Chicago

The following are ideas for pub crawls by theme and by neighborhood. Up to ten pubs have been listed per crawl, which is probably more than anyone but only the heartiest of pub crawlers can handle, so feel free to customize each route to your abilities and tastes. Regardless of their historic value, some bars have been omitted from these tours, including music venues that charge a cover to get in and other pubs where it may be problematic to host a large group of people, usually because of small size or inconvenient location.

By Theme
St. Patty's Day
Literary
Halloween
Christmas
President's Day

Special Note: Pubs on the crawls above are not within walking distance. Because driving is out of the question and taking cabs can be expensive, the use of Chicago Trolley or an equivalent form or rented transportation is highly recommended.

Chicago Trolley & Double Decker Co.
(773) 648-5000
www.chicagotrolley.com
chicagotrolley-charter@coachusa.com

BY NEIGHBORHOOD
Andersonville
Beverly
Bucktown
Edgewater
Gold Coast
Hyde Park
Jefferson Park*
Lakeview
Lincoln Park
Lincoln Square–North Center (Oktoberfest)
Little Italy–Pilsen
Logan Square–Humboldt Park
Loop–South Loop–Printers Row
Old Town
North Side*
River North
Roscoe Village
Ukrainian Village
Wicker Park
Wrigleyville
Suburban*

* Best enjoyed using Chicago Trolley or equivalent transportation method. Otherwise, the above pub crawls are designed to be on foot, sometimes finishing several blocks away from the starting point.

St. Patrick's Day Pub Crawl

to Cork & Kerry ⇓

ORDER	TAVERN	ADDRESS
A	Coogan's Riverside Saloon	180 N. Wacker Dr.
B	Shinnick's Pub	3758 S. Union Ave.
C	Cork & Kerry	10614 S. Western Ave.
D	Kitty O'Shea's	720 S. Michigan Ave.
E	Abbey Pub	3420 W. Grace St.
F	Cullen's	3741 N. Southport Ave.
G	Irish Oak	3511 N. Clark St.
H	River Shannon	425 W. Armitage Ave.
I	Brehon Pub	731 N. Wells St.
J	Butch McGuire's	20 W. Division St.

LITERARY PUB CRAWL

ORDER	TAVERN	ADDRESS
A	Gold Star Bar	1755 W. Division St.
B	California Clipper	1002 N. California Ave.
C	Lottie's Pub & Grill	1925 W. Cortland St.
D	Danny's Tavern	1951 W. Dickens Ave.
E	Sheffield's	3258 N. Sheffield Ave.
F	Green Mill	4800 N. Broadway
G	Billy Goat Tavern	430 N. Michigan Ave.
H	Woodlawn Tap	1172 E. 55th St.
I	Weeds Tavern	1555 N. Dayton St.
J	Rainbo Club	1150 N. Damen Ave.

HALLOWEEN PUB CRAWL

ORDER	TAVERN	ADDRESS
A	Webster's Wine Bar	1480 W. Webster Ave.
B	Excalibur Nightclub	632 N. Dearborn St.
C	Ethyl's Party	2600 S. Wentworth Ave.
D	Gold Star Bar	1755 W. Division St.
E	Bucktown Pub	1658 W. Cortland St.
F	Edgewater Lounge	5600 N. Ashland Ave.
G	Fireside Lounge	5739 N. Ravenswood Ave.
H	Ole St. Andrew's Inn	5938 N. Broadway
I	Guthries Tavern	1300 W. Addison St.
J	Tonic Room	2447 N. Halsted St.

CHRISTMAS PUB CRAWL

to Cork & Kerry ⇓

ORDER	TAVERN	ADDRESS
A	Signature Lounge	875 N. Michigan, 96th Fl.
B	Tavern at the Park	130 E. Randolph St.
C	Cork & Kerry	10614 S. Western Ave.
D	Lockwood	17 E. Monroe St.
E	Motel Bar	600 W. Chicago Ave.
F	Butch McGuire's	20 W. Division St.
G	River Shannon	425 W. Armitage Ave.
H	Augie's	1721 W. Wrightwood
I	Marie's Riptide Lounge	1750 W. Armitage Ave.
J	Miller's Pub	134 S. Wabash Ave.

PRESIDENT'S DAY PUB CRAWL

ORDER	TAVERN	ADDRESS
A	Poag Mahone's	175 W. Jackson St.
B	Sky Ride Lounge	105 W. Van Buren St.
C	Drum & Monkey	1435 W. Taylor St.
D	Beer Bistro	1061 W. Madison St.
E	Elephant & Castle	111 W. Adams St.
F	Jefferson Tap	325 N. Jefferson St.
G	John Barleycorn's	658 W. Belden Ave. (@ Lincoln)
H	Four Farthings	2060 N. Lincoln Ave. (@ Cleveland)
I	Weather Mark Tavern	1503 S. Michigan Ave.
J	Lockwood	17 E. Monroe St.

ANDERSONVILLE PUB CRAWL

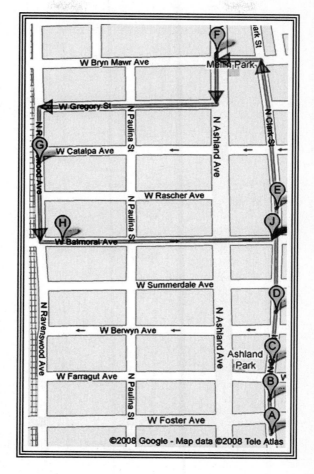

©2008 Google - Map data ©2008 Tele Atlas

ORDER	TAVERN	ADDRESS
A	Hopleaf Bar	5148 N. Clark St.
B	Konak Pizza & Grill	5150 N. Clark St.
C	Simon's Tavern	5210 N. Clark St.
D	Farragut's	5240 N. Clark St.
E	Charlie's Ale House	5308 N. Clark St.
F	In Fine Spirits	5420 N. Clark St
G	Edgewater Lounge	5600 N. Ashland Ave.
H	Ravenswood Pub	5455 N. Ravenswood Ave.
I	Joie de Vine	1744 W. Balmoral Ave.
J	Marty's Wine Bar	1511 W. Balmoral Ave.

BEVERLY PUB CRAWL

a.k.a. the "Western Walk" or "Irish Death March"

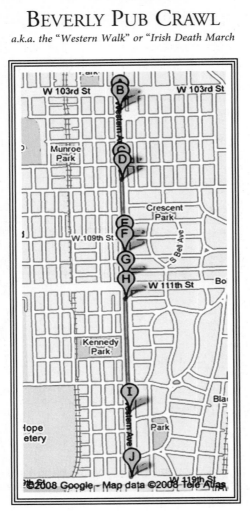

ORDER	TAVERN	ADDRESS
A	Sean's Rhino Bar	10330 S. Western Ave.
B	Brewbaker's	10350 S. Western Ave.
C	Cork & Kerry	10614 S. Western Ave.
D	Dinger's Sports Bar	10638 S. Western Ave.
E	Mrs. O'Leary's Dubliner	10910 S. Western Ave.
F	Shamrock Express	10934 S. Western Ave.
G	O'Rourke's Office	11064 S. Western Ave.
H	McNally's	11136 S. Western Ave.
I	Cullinan's Stadium Club	11610 S. Western Ave.
J	Chandler's Lounge	11848 S. Western Ave.

BUCKTOWN PUB CRAWL

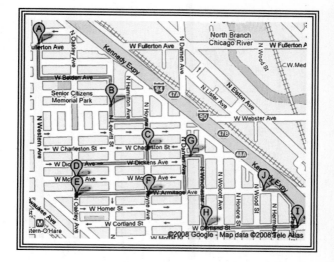

ORDER	TAVERN	ADDRESS
A	Quenchers Saloon	2401 N. Western Ave.
B	The Corner	2224 N. Leavitt St.
C	Charleston	2076 N. Hoyne Ave.
D	Gallery Cabaret	2020 N. Oakley Ave.
E	Floyd's Pub	1944 N. Oakley Ave.
F	Map Room	1949 N. Hoyne Ave.
G	Danny's Tavern	1951 W. Dickens Ave.
H	Lottie's Pub & Grill	1925 W. Cortland St.
I	Bucktown Pub	1658 W. Cortland St.
J	Marie's Riptide	1750 W. Armitage Ave.

EDGEWATER PUB CRAWL

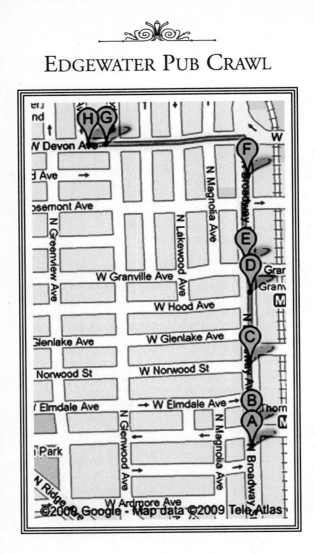

ORDER	TAVERN	ADDRESS
A	Moody's Pub	5910 N. Broadway
B	Ole St. Andrew's Inn	5938 N. Broadway
C	Double Bubble	6036 N. Broadway
D	Pumping Company	6157 N. Broadway
E	Sovereign	6202 N. Broadway
F	Hamilton's Pub	6341 N. Broadway
G	Uncommon Ground	1401 W. Devon Ave.
H	Cunneen's	1429 N. Devon Ave.

GOLD COAST PUB CRAWL

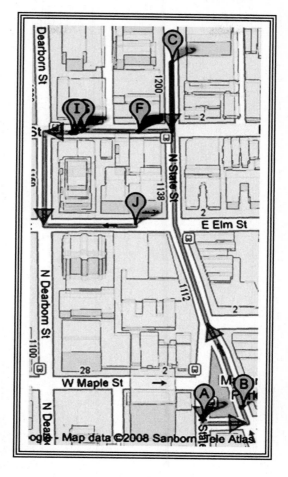

ORDER	TAVERN	ADDRESS
A	Dublin's Pub	1030 N. State St.
B	Tavern on Rush	1031 N. Rush St.
C	Zebra Lounge	1220 N. State St.
D	Leg Room	7 W. Division St.
E	Bootlegger's	13 W. Division St.
F	She-nannigan's	16 W. Division St.
G	Butch McGuire's	20 W. Division St.
H	Mother's	26 W. Division St.
I	Lodge	21 W. Division St.
J	Hangge Uppe	14 W. Elm St.

HYDE PARK PUB CRAWL

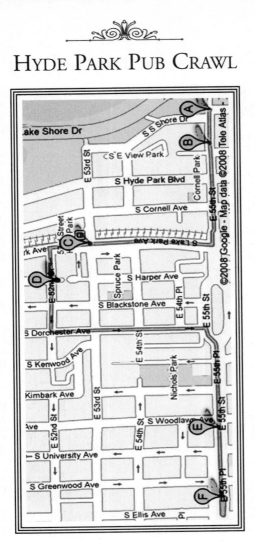

ORDER	TAVERN	ADDRESS
A	Bar Louie	5500 S. Shore Dr.
B	Cove Lounge	1750 E. 55th St.
C	Falcon Inn	1601 E. 53rd St.
D	New Checkerboard Lounge	5201 S. Harper Ct.
E	Woodlawn Tap	1172 E. 55th St.
F	Seven Ten Lanes	1055 E. 55th St.

JEFFERSON PARK PUB CRAWL

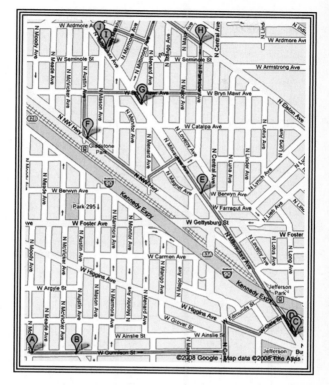

* You will need Chicago Trolley or equivalent transportation for this pub crawl.

ORDER	TAVERN	ADDRESS
A	Friendly Tavern	6124 W. Gunnison St.
B	Charlotte's Bar & Grill	6000 W. Gunnison St.
C	Jefferson Inn	4874 N. Milwaukee Ave.
D	Gale Street Inn	4914 N. Milwaukee Ave.
E	Ham Tree Inn	5333 N. Milwaukee Ave.
F	Vaughan's Pub	5485 N. Northwest Hwy.
G	Lasko's Tavern	5525 N. Milwaukee Ave.
H	Nil Tap	5734 N. Elston Ave.
I	Thatch	5707 N. Milwaukee Ave.
J	Gladstone Lounge	5734 N. Milwaukee Ave.

LAKEVIEW PUB CRAWL

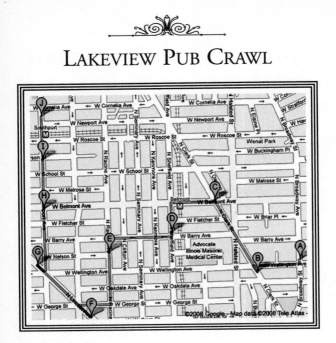

ORDER	TAVERN	ADDRESS
A	Friar Tuck	3010 N. Broadway
B	Jake's Pub	2932 N. Clark St.
C	L&L Tavern	3207 N. Clark St.
D	Matilda	3101 N. Sheffield Ave.
E	Will's Northwoods Inn	3032 N. Racine Ave.
F	Elbo Room	2871 N. Lincoln Ave.
G	Lincoln Tap Room	3010 N. Lincoln Ave.
H	Schubas Tavern	3159 N. Southport Ave.
I	Southport Lanes	3325 N. Southport Ave.
J	Mystic Celt	3443 N. Southport Ave.

LINCOLN PARK PUB CRAWL

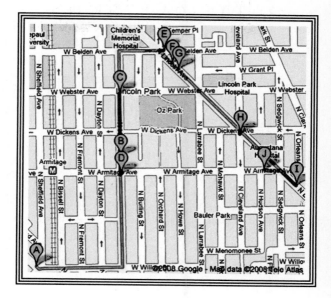

ORDER	TAVERN	ADDRESS
A	Goose Island Brew Pub	1800 N. Clybourn Ave.
B	Beaumont	2020 N. Halsted St.
C	Glascott's Groggery	2158 N. Halsted St.
D	Marquee Lounge	1973 N. Halsted St.
E	John Barleycorn's	658 W. Belden Ave.
F	Kendall's	2263 N. Lincoln Ave.
G	Sterch's	2238 N. Lincoln Ave.
H	Four Farthings	2060 N. Cleveland Ave.
I	Gamekeepers	1971 N. Lincoln Ave.
J	River Shannon	425 W. Armitage Ave.

Lincoln Square–
North Center
(and Oktoberfest)
Pub Crawl

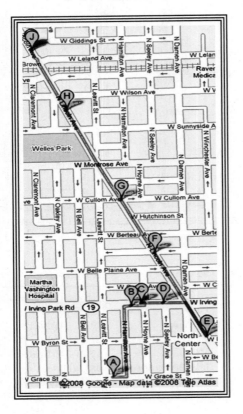

Order	Tavern	Address
A	G&L Fire Escape	2157 W. Grace Ave.
B	Laschet's Inn	2119 W. Irving Park Rd.
C	O'Donovan's	2100 W. Irving Park Rd.
D	Resi's Bierstube	2034 W. Irving Park Rd.
E	Mrs. Murphy & Sons	3905 N. Lincoln Ave.
F	Glunz Bavarian Haus	4128 N. Lincoln Ave.
G	Gannon's Pub	4264 N. Lincoln Ave.
H	Grafton Pub & Grill	4530 N. Lincoln Ave.
I	Huettenbar	4721 N. Lincoln Ave.
J	Chicago Brauhaus	4732 N. Lincoln Ave.

LITTLE ITALY–PILSEN PUB CRAWL

ORDER	TAVERN	ADDRESS
A	Hawkeye's	1458 W. Taylor St.
B	Drum & Monkey	1435 W. Taylor St.
C	Illinois Bar & Grill	1421 W. Taylor St.
D	Beviamo Wine Bar	1358 W. Taylor St.
E	Bar Louie	1321 W. Taylor St.
F	Tufano's Vernon Park Tap	1073 W. Vernon Park Pl.
G	Little Joe's Circle Lounge	1041 W. Taylor St.
H	Morgan's Bar & Grill	1325 S. Halsted St.
I	Junior's Sports Lounge	724 W. Maxwell St.
J	Skylark	2149 S. Halsted St.

LOGAN SQUARE–HUMBOLDT PARK PUB CRAWL

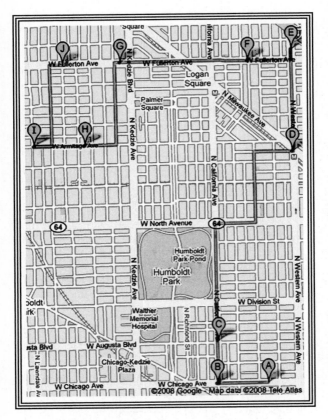

* You will need Chicago Trolley or equivalent transportation for this pub crawl.

ORDER	TAVERN	ADDRESS
A	Black Beetle	2532 W. Chicago Ave.
B	Continental	2801 W. Chicago Ave.
C	California Clipper	1002 N. California Ave.
D	Green Eye Lounge	2403 W. Homer Ave.
E	Mutiny	2428 N. Western Ave.
F	Bob Inn	2609 W. Fullerton Ave.
G	Whirlaway	3224 W. Fullerton Ave.
H	Rosa's Lounge	3420 W. Armitage Ave.
I	Weegee's Lounge	3659 W. Armitage Ave.
J	Hotti Biscotti	3545 W. Fullerton Ave.

LOOP–SOUTH LOOP–
PRINTERS ROW PUB CRAWL

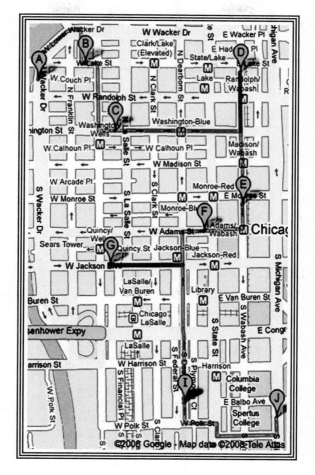

ORDER	TAVERN	ADDRESS
A	Coogan's Riverside Saloon	180 N. Wacker Dr.
B	Monk's Pub	205 W. Lake St.
C	Cardozo's Pub	170 W. Washington St.
D	Elephant & Castle	185 N. Wabash Ave.
E	Miller's Pub	134 S. Wabash Ave.
F	17 West at the Berghoff	17 W. Adams St.
G	Poag Mahone's	175 W. Jackson Blvd.
H	Kasey's Tavern	701 S. Dearborn St.
I	Hackney's	733 S. Dearborn St.
J	Kitty O'Shea's	720 S. Michigan Ave.

NORTH SIDE PUB CRAWL

* You will need Chicago Trolley or equivalent
  transportation for this pub crawl.

ORDER	TAVERN	ADDRESS
A	Emmit's Pub	495 N. Milwaukee Ave.
B	Hideout	1354 W. Wabansia Ave.
C	Mirabell	3454 W. Addison St.
D	Abbey Pub	3420 W. Grace St.
E	Cunneen's	1438 W. Devon Ave.
F	Heartland Café	7000 N. Glenwood Ave.
G	Fireside	5739 N. Ravenswood Ave.
H	Carol's Pub	4659 N. Clark St.
I	Weeds Tavern	1555 N. Dayton St.
J	Silver Palm & Matchbox	768–770 N. Milwaukee Ave.

OLD TOWN PUB CRAWL

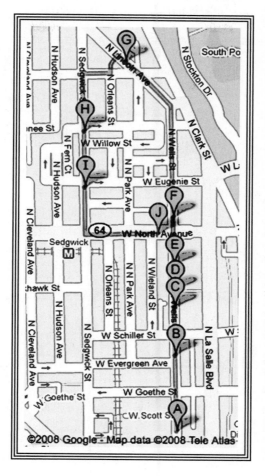

@2008 Google - Map data ©2008 Tele Atlas

ORDER	TAVERN	ADDRESS
A	Saluki Bar	1208 N. Wells St.
B	Old Town Pub	1339 N. Wells St.
C	Burton Place	1447 N. Wells St.
D	Fireplace Inn	1448 N. Wells St.
E	O'Brien's Restaurant & Bar	1528 N. Wells St.
F	Old Town Ale House	219 W. North Ave.
G	Corcoran's Grill & Pub	1615 N. Wells St.
H	Bricks	1909 N. Lincoln Ave.
I	Marge's Still	1758 N. Sedgwick St.
J	Twin Anchors	1655 N. Sedgwick St.

RIVER NORTH–MAGNIFICENT MILE PUB CRAWL

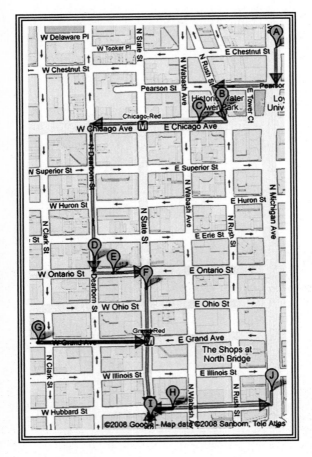

ORDER	TAVERN	ADDRESS
A	Signature Lounge	875 N. Michigan Ave.
B	Pippin's Tavern	806 N. Rush St.
C	Streeter's Tavern	50 E. Chicago Ave.
D	Excalibur Nightclub	632 N. Dearborn St.
E	Redhead Piano Bar	16 W. Ontario St.
F	Pops for Champagne	601 N. State St.
G	Fadó Irish Pub	100 W. Grand Ave.
H	Andy's Jazz Club	11 E. Hubbard St.
I	Rossi's Liquors	412 N. State St.
J	Billy Goat Tavern	430 N. Michigan Ave.

ROSCOE VILLAGE PUB CRAWL

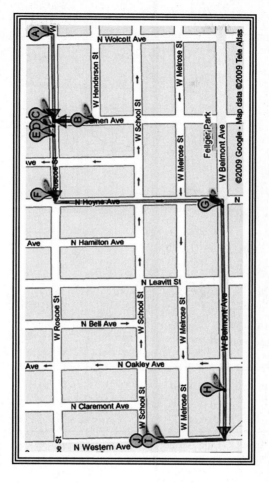

ORDER	TAVERN	ADDRESS
A	Four Moon Tavern	1847 W. Roscoe St.
B	Four Treys	3333 N. Damen Ave.
C	Riverview Tavern	1958 W. Roscoe St.
D	Mulligan's	2000 W. Roscoe St.
E	Volo	2008 W. Roscoe St.
F	Village Tap	2055 W. Roscoe St.
G	Beat Kitchen	2100 W. Belmont Ave.
H	Hungry Brain	2319 W. Belmont Ave.
I	Underbar	3243 N. Western Ave.
J	Bluelight	3251 N. Western Ave.

UKRANIAN VILLAGE PUB CRAWL

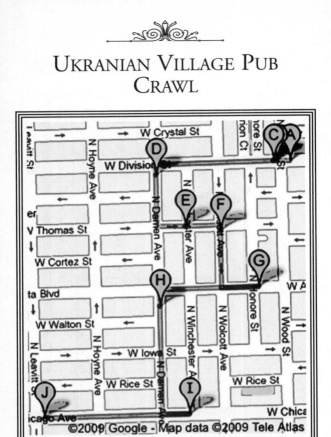

ORDER	TAVERN	ADDRESS
A	Gold Star Bar	1755 W. Division St.
B	Phyllis' Musical Inn	1800 W. Division St.
C	Smoke Daddy	1804 W. Division St.
D	Rainbo Club	1150 N. Damen Ave.
E	Inner Town Pub	1935 W. Thomas St.
F	Happy Village	1059 N. Wolcott Ave.
G	Club Foot	1824 W. Augusta Blvd.
H	Ola's Liquors	947 N. Damen Ave.
I	Cleo's	1935 W. Chicago Ave.
J	Tuman's	2159 W. Chicago Ave.

WICKER PARK PUB CRAWL

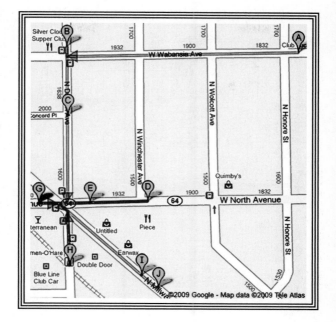

ORDER	TAVERN	ADDRESS
A	Club Lucky	1824 W. Wabansia Ave.
B	Silver Cloud	1700 N. Damen Ave.
C	Northside Bar & Grill	1635 N. Damen Ave.
D	Piece	1927 W. North Ave.
E	Wicker Park Tavern	1958 W. North Ave.
F	Estelle's	2013 W. North Ave.
G	Subterranean	2011 W. North Ave.
H	Blue Line Lounge	1548 N. Damen Ave.
I	Pint	1547 N. Milwaukee Ave.
J	Nick's Beergarden	1516 N. Milwaukee Ave.

WRIGLEYVILLE PUB CRAWL

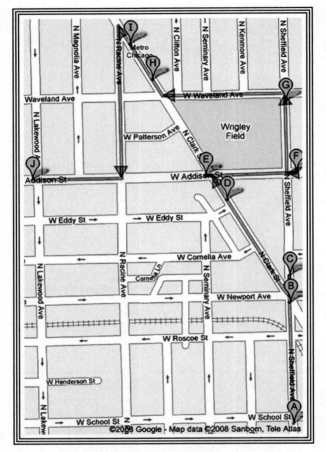

* On this pub crawl, you will encounter several more bars in between the suggested bars highlighted.

ORDER	TAVERN	ADDRESS
A	Sheffield's	3258 N. Sheffield Ave.
B	Blarney Stone	3424 N. Sheffield Ave.
C	Nisei Lounge	3439 N. Sheffield Ave.
D	Sluggers	3540 N. Clark St.
E	Cubby Bear	1059 W. Addison St.
F	The Dugout	950 W. Addison St.
G	Murphy's Bleachers	3655 N. Sheffield Ave.
H	Yak-zies on Clark	3710 N. Clark St.
I	Gingerman	3740 N. Clark St.
J	Guthries Tavern	1300 W. Addison St.

SUBURBAN PUB CRAWL

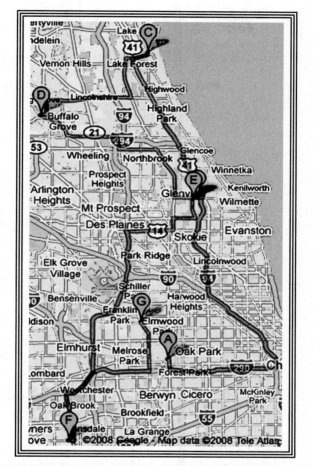

* For obvious reasons, you will need Chicago Trolley or
equivalent transportation for this pub crawl.

ORDER	TAVERN	ADDRESS
A	Goldyburgers	7316 Circle Ave. (Forest Park)
B	Meier's Tavern	235 E. Lake St. (Glenview)
C	The Lantern	768 N. Western (Lake Forest)
D	Village Tavern	135 Old McHenry (Long Grove)
E	Hackney's	1241 Harms Rd. (Glenview)
F	Country House	241 W. 55th St. (Clarendon Hills)
G	Hala Kahiki	2834 River Rd. (River Grove)

"Yet once you've come to be part of this particular patch, you'll never love another. Like loving a woman with a broken nose, you may well find lovelier lovelies. But never a lovely so real."

"By nights when the yellow salamanders of the El bend all one way and the cold rain runs with the red-lit rain. By the way the city's million wires are burdened only by lightest snow; and the old year yet lighter upon them. When chairs are stacked and glasses are turned and arc lamps all are dimmed. By days when the wind bangs alley gates ajar and the sun goes by on the wind. By nights when the moon is an old child above the measured thunder of the cars, you may know Chicago's heart at last."

—Nelson Algren, *Chicago: City on the Make* (1951)

INDEXES

BY YEAR OPENED

Wolf Tavern
1829

Village Tavern
1849

Schaller's Pump
1881

Marge's Still
1885

17 West at the Berghoff
1898

Green Mill Cocktail Lounge
1907

Kasey's Tavern
1914

Green Door Tavern
1921

Country House
1922

Southport Lanes & Billiards
1922

Tufanos Vernon Park Tap
1930

Burwood Tap
1933

Coq d'Or
1933

Guthries Tavern
1933

Hamilton's Pub
1933

Jake's Pub
1933

Kelly's Pub
1933

Twin Anchors
1933

Zebra Lounge
1933

Billy Goat Tavern
1934

Durkin's
1934

Gold Star Bar
1934

Hideout
1934

Lincoln Tavern
1934

Simon's Tavern
1934

Miller's Pub
1935

Rainbo Club
1936

California Clipper
1937

Glascott's Groggery
1937

Pump Room
1938

Shinnick's Pub
1938

Hackney's
1939

Woodlawn Tap
1944

Matchbox
1945

River Shannon
1946

Jazz Showcase
1947

By Year Opened

Theresa's Lounge
1949

Beachwood Inn
1950

Nisei Lounge
1950

Andy's Jazz Club
1951

Club Lago
1952

Cubby Bear
1953

Phyllis' Musical Inn
1954

The Lodge
1957

Old Town Ale House
1958

Moody's Pub
1959

Playboy Club
1960

Butch McGuire's
1961

Marie's Riptide Lounge
1961

Gale Street Inn
1963

Resi's Bierstube
1964

Weeds Tavern
1964

Chicago Brauhaus
1965

Cove Lounge
1965

Hala Kahiki
1965

John Barleycorn Memorial Pub
1965

Fireplace Inn
1966

Four Farthings Tavern & Grill
1968

Kingston Mines
1968

Mother's
1968

Wise Fools Pub
1968

Half Shell
1969

Monk's Pub
1969

BackRoom
1970

Edgewater Lounge
1970

Friar Tuck
1970

New Apartment Lounge
1970

Laschet's Inn
1971

Sterch's
1971

New Checkerboard Lounge
1972

Carol's Pub
1973

Hangge Uppe
1973

Abbey Pub
1974

Cunneen's
1974

Heartland Café
1976

Gingerman
1977

Mirabell Restaurant & Lounge
1977

Nick's Beergarden
1977

B.L.U.E.S.
1979

Neo
1979

BY YEAR OPENED

Quenchers Saloon
1979

Beaumont
1980

Brehon Pub
1980

Murphy's Bleachers
1980

Sheffield's Beer & Wine Garden
1980

Whirlaway
1980

Coogan's Riverside Saloon
1982

New Velvet Lounge
1982

Pops for Champagne
1982

Red Lion Pub
1984

Rosa's Lounge
1984

L&L Tavern
1985

Kitty O'Shea's
1986

Local Option
1986

Lottie's Pub & Grill
1986

Sluggers
1986

Lounge Axe
1987

Cork & Kerry
1988

Goose Island Brew Pub
1988

Buddy Guy's Legends
1989

Elbo Room
1989

Excalibur Nightclub
1989

Schubas Tavern
1989

Club Lucky
1990

Fireside
1990

Mutiny
1990

Yak-zies on Clark
1990

Signature Lounge
1993

Webster's Wine Bar
1994

Walter Payton's Roundhouse
1995

BY TYPE

Mirabell Restaurant & Lounge
Austrian Restaurant

B.L.U.E.S.
Blues Club

Buddy Guy's Legends
Blues Club

Kingston Mines
Blues Club

New Checkerboard Lounge
Blues Club

Rosa's Lounge
Blues Club

Theresa's Lounge
Blues Club

Goose Island Brew Pub
Brew Pub

Walter Payton's Roundhouse
Brew Pub

Club Lucky
Cocktail Lounge

Playboy Club
Cocktail Lounge

Signature Lounge
Cocktail Lounge

Carol's Pub
Country Bar

Cove Lounge
Dive Bar

Half Shell
Dive Bar

Marie's Riptide Lounge
Dive Bar

Monk's Pub
Dive Bar

Mutiny
Dive Bar

Nick's Beergarden
Dive Bar

Phyllis' Musical Inn
Dive Bar

Rainbo Club
Dive Bar

Weeds Tavern
Dive Bar

Red Lion Pub
English Pub

17 West at the Berghoff
German Bar/Restaurant

Chicago Brauhaus
German Bar/Restaurant

Laschet's Inn
German Bar/Restaurant

Resi's Bierstube
German Bar/Restaurant

Coq d'Or
Hotel Bar

Kitty O'Shea's
Hotel Bar

Pump Room
Hotel Bar

Abbey Pub
Irish Pub

Coogan's Riverside Saloon
Irish Pub

Cork & Kerry
Irish Pub

Tufano's Vernon Park Tap
Italian Joint

Andy's Jazz Club
Jazz Club

BackRoom
Jazz Club

Green Mill Cocktail Lounge
Jazz Club

Jazz Showcase
Jazz Club

New Apartment Lounge
Jazz Club

New Velvet Lounge
Jazz Club

Pops for Champagne
Jazz Club

Beaumont
Meat Market

The Lodge
Meat Market

Mother's
Meat Market

By Type

By Type

Sheffield's Beer & Wine Garden
Neighborhood Tavern

Shinnick's Pub
Neighborhood Tavern

Simon's Tavern
Neighborhood Tavern

Southport Lanes & Billiards
Neighborhood Tavern

Sterch's
Neighborhood Tavern

Twin Anchors
Neighborhood Tavern

Village Tavern
Neighborhood Tavern

Whirlaway
Neighborhood Tavern

Wolf Tavern
Neighborhood Tavern

Woodlawn Tap
Neighborhood Tavern

Excalibur Nightclub
Nightclub

Hangge Uppe
Nightclub

Neo
Nightclub

Zebra Lounge
Piano Lounge

Gale Street Inn
Rib Joint

Country House
Roadhouse

Cubby Bear
Sports Bar

Murphy's Bleachers
Sports Bar

Sluggers
Sports Bar

Yak-zies on Clark
Sports Bar

Hala Kahiki
Tiki Bar

Webster's Wine Bar
Wine Bar

By Page

By Page

By Page

By Page

BY PAGE

V

Village Tavern
210–211

W

Walter Payton's Roundhouse
212–213

Webster's Wine Bar
188–189

Weeds Tavern
190–191

Whirlaway
192–193

Wicker Park Pub Crawl
257

Wise Fools Pub
194–195

Wolf Tavern
220–221

Woodlawn Tap
196–197

Wrigleyville Pub Crawl
258

Y

Yak-Zies on Clark
198–199

Z

Zebra Lounge
200–201

Founded in 1994, LAKE CLAREMONT PRESS specializes in books on the Chicago area and its history, focusing on preserving the city's past, exploring its present environment, and cultivating a strong sense of place for the future. Visit us on the web at www.lakeclaremont.com.

SELECTED BOOKLIST

A Chicago Tavern: A Goat, a Curse, and the American Dream

Hollywood on Lake Michigan: Chicago and the Movies

The Beat Cop's Guide to Chicago Eats

A Cook's Guide to Chicago

Carless in Chicago

Oldest Chicago

Graveyards of Chicago

The Chicago River Architecture Tour

The Chicago River: A Natural and Unnatural History

From Lumber Hookers to the Hooligan Fleet:
A Treasury of Chicago Maritime History

Rule 53: Capturing Hippies, Spies, Politicians,
and Murderers in an American Courtroom

On the Job: Behind the Stars of the Chicago Police Department

For Members Only: A History and Guide to Chicago's
Oldest Private Clubs

Today's Chicago Blues

Finding Your Chicago Irish

Finding Your Chicago Ancestors: A Beginner's Guide
to Family History in the City and Cook County